Let the Children Come and Worship

Little Liturgies for Young Christians

Judy Gattis Smith

CSS Publishing Company, Inc.
Lima, Ohio

LET THE CHILDREN COME AND WORSHIP

For more information about CSS Publishing Company resources, visit our website at www.csspub.com, email us at csr@csspub.com, or call (800) 241-4056.

e-book:
ISBN-13: 978-0-7880-2812-0
ISBN-10: 0-7880-2812-X

ISBN-13: 978-0-7880-2811-3
ISBN-10: 0-7880-2811-1   PRINTED IN USA

*For Tammy Tipton-Nay
and the children of Brandermill Church*

Author's Update

All of these liturgies were experienced and critiqued by children in a variety of settings. Their ideas were incorporated in each final production. Since the first publication of these liturgies our culture and our churches have changed. We are more sensitive about always speaking of God in the masculine gender. However, I have kept the original language I first used. Feel free to change this.

Also the songs and hymns that were popular with children when these liturgies were first written may not be as familiar to today's children. Again, adjust these liturgies to your particular situation and location. These are just vehicles to help children experience God.

The children who first experienced and critiqued these liturgies are now adults. It is my hope that many of them are teaching Sunday school and working with children in their own churches.

Table of Contents

Introduction

Deep inside every person is a basic need to celebrate, to worship. This need is present from the very beginning of our lives.

Children are a part of the worshiping community but often a forgotten part. Our services of worship, Sunday after Sunday, are geared specifically to adults. The words, both written and spoken, the movements and the symbols are often foreign to a child's understanding. But children, as well as learning and studying about God, should have the experience of meeting God. Worship should not be put off until they can understand and identify with adult liturgy.

Contained in the following pages are services written specifically for children's worship. Other age levels are welcome and encouraged to join the worship experience, but the focus is on the interests and expressions of children. The elements that we associate with worship are present: praise of God, prayers for forgiveness, affirmation of faith, and dedication of lives. But the form may seem strange.

"The Spirit blows where it will" and no one can guarantee when the divine presence will break through in a human situation. But these liturgies are based on the belief and expectation that God will come to all his children, even the young ones, if we sincerely prepare and await his presence.

The belief is inherent in this liturgy that God loves children as they are and if they turn to him, there he is in their midst, laughing and celebrating with them, drying their small tears, enlarging their world of pets, school, and family with his presence.

Let the children come — and worship God.

A Better Way

Preparation for the Service

A celebration of the family and suggestions for living in a family group are the themes of this children's liturgy. In using this liturgy be sensitive to the fact that not all children live in traditional families. Adapt this to the situation in your local congregation.

To Prepare

1. Have sheets of a genealogical tree (can be found online) and pencils for each member of the congregation.
2. Select child readers for the scriptures.
3. Have children make simple hand puppets; one serving dish will be held by a puppet. They will also need yarn and fake fur.
4. Rehearse sermon/puppet show with reader and four puppet characters.

Order of Service

Prelude

Welcome

Hymn: "Happy The Home When God Is There"

Prayer Meditation with Trees

Scripture

Song: "They'll Know We Are Christians By Our Love"

Sermon/Puppet Show

Dedication Prayer

Closing Hymn: "Blest Be The Tie That Binds"

Leader: Welcome to our children's liturgy. We are here today to thank God for homes and families. We thank him for all the people in our family: mothers and fathers who take care of us, brothers and sisters to play and share with us. Home is a place where there is good, warm food to help us grow healthy and strong. It is a place where we can find a comfortable bed after a long, tiring day. It is a place where we can laugh. It is a place where we can cry. It is a place where we can feel secure and protected. How thoughtful of God to place us in families!

Hymn: "Happy The Home When God Is There"

Leader: As you came in, you were given a picture of a tree. We want to use these trees to focus our prayer time together today. Will each of you write your name on the trunk of your tree? When this is completed please bow your heads.

Here we are Lord, some of the trees in your forest. Help us weather the storms, enjoy the sunshine, give shelter and comfort to others, just like a tree. We ask your blessing on us as we each now say our own name silently before you. Amen.

Your tree has roots. Will you now write on these roots the names of all the members of your family: mother, father, brothers and sisters, and grandparents. When completed please bow your heads.

Father, we are so grateful for these members of our family. We ask your blessing on each of them as we say their names silently now before you. Amen.

Your tree has branches. Will you now write the names of some of the other people who are important in your life on these branches: friends, neighbors, teachers. When completed please bow your heads.

Father, we are grateful for all these other people whose lives touch ours. We ask your blessing on each one of them as we say their names silently before you now. Amen.

The ushers will now collect our trees and bring them to the altar.

Dear God you are Father of us all. We all belong to your family. We are all trees in your forest. For everyone in the whole human family we pray. Amen.

(Ushers put up trees with tape or clip to wires, simulating a forest of trees.)

Leader: The Bible is full of advice for us about how we should live in families. Let's listen to some of this advice now.
Child Reader: Exodus 20:12
Child Reader: Colossians 3:12-14, 20-21
Child Reader: Luke 2:41-51

Song: "They'll Know We Are Christians By Our Love"

Sermon/Puppet Show
We have been thanking God that we live in families with parents to care for us and brothers and sisters to play with. But living in a family sometimes means conflicts. Sometimes we fight with our brothers and sisters. Sometimes our parents make us angry. If there has been a fuss or a fight in our family sometimes we feel we are to blame and we feel very guilty. The Bible tells us over and over that those of us living in families must learn forgiveness. Just as God forgives us when we do wrong so we must forgive members of our family when they wrong us.

We are going to hear a Bible story today that tells us about a quarrel in a family. The Bible, as you know, is about real people who faced some of the same problems we face.

Our story takes place many years ago, in a family. The father of the family was named Isaac.

(*Puppet appears, points to self, bows*)

The mother was named Rebekah.

(*Puppet appears, points to self, bows*)

Isaac and Rebekah wanted a son very badly. They were over-joyed when they had not one son — but two — twin boys whom they named Jacob and Esau.

(*Puppets appear, point to selves, bow*)

Esau grew up to be an outdoors man, a skillful hunter and trapper. Jacob was quiet, preferring to stay indoors. The Bible says: "Isaac loved Esau but Rebekah loved Jacob."

(*Isaac puts arm around Esau, Rebekah puts arm around Jacob*)

(*Puppets go offstage*)

Finally Isaac grew very old. His eyesight dimmed until he could barely see.

(*Isaac comes tottering on stage*)

He called his favorite son Esau to him.

(*Waves hand toward body*)

(*Esau appears*)

Isaac told Esau that he was getting very old and the time had come for him to give to his son all his lands, all his cattle and most importantly, his special blessing. But first, he said, "Take your bow and arrow and go kill some game for me and cook it your special way for I do love your cooking."

(*Esau nods in agreement and leaves*)

(*Isaac leaves*)

But, unknown to Isaac, Rebekah had overheard the conversation.

(Rebekah comes up, looks around)

"It's not fair!" she thought. "Jacob is smarter. He should not be left out in the cold. If Esau gets the special blessing Jacob will have nothing. Esau likes hunting and out-of-doors. He can always take care of himself. But what will happen to poor Jacob?"

Then she had an idea.

(Rubs hands together to express cunning)

She called Jacob and told him her plan.

(Jacob appears, puppets bend heads toward each other to suggest talking together)

"While Esau is out hunting," she said, "I'll make some stew out of goat meat and you can take it in to Isaac and he'll bless you instead of Esau."

(Rebekah brings up large, oversized dish)

"Here it is, all simmering and bubbling just the way he likes it." But Jacob shook his head.

(Puppet rotates back and forth to express negative idea)

"I don't think this is going to work. Esau is hairy and I am not. What if he feels my hands and arms and figures out it is me, not Esau?"

Rebekah had another idea.

(Taps head lightly with one hand to express thinking)

(Rebekah pops below and brings up yarn. She puts it on Jacob)

Rebekah took some of the skin from the goat and put it on Jacob's arms and neck. Then she dressed him in Esau's clothes.

(*Drapes skin around him*)

"Now, he'll never know the difference."

(*Rebekah leaves*)

So Jacob, dressed as Esau, took the food and went in to Isaac to be blessed.

(*Jacob bows before Isaac*)

"Here I am, father, give me your blessing."

"You sound like Jacob," Isaac said. "Let me feel your arms."

(*Puppet feels other puppet*)

"Well, I guess you are Esau. I can't see very well, you know. Here is my blessing to you."

(*Places hand on Jacob's head, Jacob bows*)

"Now all that I have is yours."

(*Isaac leaves*)

Jacob and Rebekah were very happy. The blessing was Jacob's.

(*Puppets express joy by clapping hands and dancing together*)

After a while Esau returned.

(*Puppet appears*)

When he learned about the trick that had been played on him, he let out an angry scream and vowed to get even with Jacob.

(Esau waves arms in anger)

Poor Jacob was very frightened.

(Puppet trembles)

He was afraid Esau would murder him for what he had done.

So, all alone, Jacob sneaked away from his home.

(Puppet turns and waves good-bye)

He walked and he ran, always afraid of being followed.

(Puppet moves up and down in a choppy manner while crossing stage to give illusion of running)

His feet were bruised from the stones and his eyes ached from the sun and dust. Jacob realized he had done a wicked thing. Although he had his father's blessing he was alone in a strange country with no mother, no father, and no brother.

(Puppet leaves)

What would have happened if there had been forgiveness in the family?

Isaac, come here.

(Puppet appears)

The story would have ended differently if you had forgiven Jacob for not being strong and manly like Esau and shared your inheritance with both of them.

(Puppet bows head to floor in shame)

Rebekah, come here.

(Puppet appears)

The story would have ended differently if you had forgiven Esau for not being as smart or as handsome as Jacob and if you had talked to Isaac about sharing the inheritance instead of trying to trick him.

(*Puppet bows head to floor*)

Jacob and Esau, come here.

(*Puppets appear*)

You needed to learn how to live in a family too. Living in a family means not only doing things for others but trying to understand each other and then accepting what we cannot understand without blame.

All the characters in this story suffered because they had not acted in a loving manner.

(*Puppets leave*)

Prayer
O loving Father, bless our home that we may all be happy in your love. Help us to be ready to help and quick to forgive, sharing our joys and comforting our sorrows. May your loving spirit rule our hearts and lips by the law of kindness. O loving Father, make us all your true and happy children and fill our homes with the gladness of your presence.

Leader: Will the children go now into the congregation and get their parents and bring them to the altar? Here let us form a circle and sing "Blest Be The Tie That Binds."

Children, Let Us Pray

Preparation for the Service

This children's liturgy looks at the ways in which we pray. Children are given the actual experience of prayer in a variety of ways within the Christian community.

To Prepare

1. Choose a child reader for scripture.

2. Arrange for use of a cymbal and a stringed instrument. Rehearse the responsive reading with them.

3. Choose a storyteller for the participation story.

4. Choose someone to teach and lead the round "For Health And Strength And Daily Food." And to also lead the movement song "Praise Ye The Lord, Alleluia."

Order of Service

Opening Remarks

Scripture

Song: "Kum Ba Yah"

Prayers of Adoration

Song: "Praise Him! Praise Him! All Ye Little Children"

Responsive Sentences

Song: "Praise Ye The Lord, Alleluia"

Responsive Reading with Instruments

Prayers of Confession
Song: "Standing In The Need Of Prayer"

Prayers of Thanksgiving
Silent Prayers with Forgiveness
Song: "For Health And Strength And Daily Food" (sung in round)

Prayers of Petition
Donald Soper's Prayer

Participation Story: Friend Who Came at Midnight

Prayers for Others

Lord's Prayer

Song: "I'm Gonna Sing When Spirit Says Sing"

Leader: Welcome to our children's liturgy. We have come together today to pray and to learn about prayer. Jesus prayed often. Listen to what our scriptures say:

Child Reader:

Luke 4:16 — Jesus prayed in the synagogue.

Luke 5:16 — Jesus prayed all night on the hillside.

Luke 22:39-41 — Jesus prayed in a garden.

Song: "Kum Ba Yah" (someone's praying verse)

Leader: There are many kinds of prayers from the smallest requests to the grandest thanksgiving, and we believe God hears all of our prayers. Today in our worship we are going to look at four kinds of prayers.

Our first prayers will be prayers of adoration to God. We praise our Creator!

Stand and sing: "Praise Him! Praise Him! All Ye Little Children"

Leader: O magnify the Lord with me and let us praise his name.

Boys: The prophets praised him.

Girls: The disciples praised him.

All: The church praised him.

Boys: Boys praise him.

Girls: Girls praise him.

All: We praise him and glorify his name.

Hymn: "Praise Ye The Lord, Alleluia"

(*clash of cymbal*)

Minister: Do you hear that cymbal?

People: Yes, we hear that cymbal.

Minister: Praise the Lord with cymbals.

People: Praise him with loud cymbals.

Minister: O sing unto the Lord a new song.
(*sound of stringed instrument*)
Minister: Do you hear that stringed instrument?
People: Yes, we hear that stringed instrument.
Minister: Make a joyful noise unto the Lord.
People: Praise God for all his blessings to us.
Minister: Praise him for his noble acts.
People: Praise him for every living thing.
Minister: Sing unto the Lord.
People: Sing praise unto the Lord.
Doxology: "Praise God From Whom All Blessings Flow"

Leader: Our next prayers are prayers of confession. None of us has been as good as we might have been. We have all done things for which we are truly sorry. Maybe we cheated on a test, took something that didn't belong to us, told a lie, hurt someone, or made fun of someone. We want to admit our wrongs and ask God's forgiveness.

To show God how we feel let's all kneel. Now will you bow your heads and shut your eyes and fold your hands in prayer? In this position we show our helplessness before God and ask for his mercy.

Think silently of the things you have done wrong and ask forgiveness for each one. (*pause*)

Now will you silently ask God's help in changing one thing about your life? (*pause*) All rise and take your seats.

We are all God's children and he loves us. He forgives us for our wrongdoing and he will help us to be the strong, good children we are meant to be. Listen to what God says to us in Psalm 103:11-12: "For as the heavens are high above the earth, so great is his steadfast love toward those who fear him; as far as the east is from the west, so far he removes our transgressions from us."

Isn't that a wonderful promise? Don't feel guilty any more. God forgives you whatever you have done. Your mistake has gone as far as the east from the west and God's love for you is as high as the heavens.

Song: "Standing In The Need Of Prayer"

Leader: Our next prayers are prayers of thanksgiving. God has given us so much and there are so many things that we just want to say "thank you" for. Let's think together now about some of these things.

What are some of your favorite foods? (*children call out answers and leader collects them into a short prayer*)

Leader: For pizza and ice cream and good fresh milk, for fresh bread and donuts (or whatever), thank you, God!

Leader: What are your favorite animals? (*children call out answers*)

Leader: For gerbils and puppies and horses and mice (or whatever), thank you, God!

Leader: Who is your favorite friend? (*children call out answers*)

Leader: For Amy and Brett and Robert and Kim (or whomever), thank you, God!

Leader: What is your favorite flower? (*accept answers*)

Leader: For roses and buttercups and marigolds and violets, thank you, God!

Leader: What is your favorite game? (*accept answers*)

Leader: For basketball and soccer and kickball and checkers, thank you, God!

Leader: What is your favorite weather? (*accept answers*)

Leader: For snow and ice and springtime and fall, thank you, God!

Song: "For Health And Strength And Daily Food" (sung in round)

Leader: Our fourth prayers are prayers of petition in which we ask God for something for ourselves or for another. The shortest prayer in the Bible is a prayer of petition: Matthew 15:25: "Lord, help me!"

Here is another famous prayer:

"Help me, O God, to believe that whatever it is that I want or need I ought to tell you about it, and that I ought also to believe that you will answer my prayer, even though your answer may be different from the one I hope for. So shall I be your loving and trusting child and all things will work together for good."

— Donald Soper

It's all right to ask God for things when we pray. Just as our own father likes to give us good things because he loves us, so our heavenly Father loves to give us good things. Of course, it would be greedy and selfish to always be asking for things; but Jesus said we should ask God for things when we pray and he even told a story about it. Let's listen to the story now. Will you help me tell it by making some of the sounds? (divide congregation into three groups)

Group 1: knocking sound on seats

Group 2: snoring, sleeping sounds

Group 3: footsteps (*running, walking, tip-toeing*)

(*practice sounds*)

(Leader tells story and indicates when groups are to make sounds.)

Friend Who Came at Midnight

Leader: In a Jewish household in the time of our story the people did not keep time as we do today. Instead of clocks, they lived by the sun. They went to bed soon after it was dark and got up after the sun rose. They divided the night into four parts. They went to bed in the evening (between 6 and 9 o'clock). From about 9 p.m. to 12 a.m. they called midnight.

Then came the three hours called "cockcrow," and at about 3 a.m. began the three hours called dawn.

On the night of our story, the sun had gone down and the family was getting ready for bed. Let's listen to how it would have sounded.

First there were the running footsteps of the animals as they were herded indoors and settled down for the night.
(Group 3)
Then the slower footsteps of the children as they brought out their mats which had been rolled up and put away in a corner.
(Group 2)
Suddenly there came a loud banging on the door.
(Group 1)
Who on earth could it be at this hour of the night? There must be something wrong. No one ever disturbed the peace of the night in the little village. The father woke immediately and looked around. The children were still asleep.
(Group 2)
"Who is it? What do you want?"
"It is your friend," came the answer. "I am on a journey and need food and shelter for the night." Now all the family and animals were awake and stirring about.
(Group 3)
The friend was welcomed gladly. There were many dangers for a traveler in those days. A man could die of thirst in the heat. Shelter from the bitter cold of the night was important too. Robbers hid behind rocks and wild animals roamed the countryside. So it was a sacred duty to welcome visitors and give them food and shelter. A man could easily die if he were turned away. The friend's hands and face and dusty feet were washed and they all sat down, ready to eat, drink, and talk.

Then a terrible thing happened. The mother discovered that there was no bread in the house. It had all been eaten at supper. There was no food for the hungry visitor! This

was not just rude and unkind, but was breaking the sacred law. There was only one thing to do — borrow bread from a neighbor. The father tiptoed out of the house.
(Group 3)
He wrapped his cloak around him and headed for his neighbor's house.
(Group 3)
Next door the neighbor's family was sleeping soundly.
(Group 2)
When he reached the house he knocked on the door.
(Group 1)
Inside, the father was startled out of a deep sleep. What was that terrible noise? Was it only a dream? The knocking came again.
(Group 1)
Perhaps if he kept quiet it would go away. Besides, if he called out he would wake his family. He pulled the covers over his head. But it was no use. The banging went on.
(Group 1)
Now someone was calling his name. "Neighbor! Neighbor! Wake up!" The father looked at his sleeping family.
(Group 2)
"Go away," he said.
"I have a visitor. He has been on the road all day. He needs food," called the neighbor, and the knocking came again.
(Group 1)
"Everyone here is asleep. Go away."
(Group 2)
But the banging still went on.
(Group 1)
"I must have bread! I'll pay you back tomorrow." The neighbor didn't want to get up at that time of night. He would have to wake up the whole family to get the bread, as well as disturbing the animals. They might mill around, upset, for the rest of the night.

(Group 3)
But the neighbor would not give up. He went on banging at the door. He just would not stop knocking and calling out for the bread.
(Group 1)
When the neighbor saw it was no use, he woke his family from their sleep.
(Group 2)
He moved all the mats to get to the bread. This disturbed the animals and they begin pushing and milling.
(Group 3)
He took the bar off the door and thrust the loaves into the hands of his friend. The neighbor thanked him and hurried back to the house carrying the bread for the needy traveler.
(Group 3)
He had gotten what he wanted by persisting — by keeping on asking. There was a happy feast in his house that night. Next door the neighbors finally settled back to sleep.*
(Group 2)
Jesus told this story to tell us that we could always ask God for things and that we should keep on asking.

We can also ask for things for others. We can ask God's blessing on our country and its leaders. We can pray for our church. We can pray for our family and friends. We can pray for those who are sick.

Let's each now think silently of one person — a friend, brother, or sister. Name that person silently before God and pray for him.

(*pause*)

When Jesus' disciples asked him how to pray he gave them an example that we call The Lord's Prayer. To conclude our worship today, let's all join in saying this prayer together.

Our Father, who art in heaven hallowed be thy name. Thy kingdom come, thy will be done, on earth as it is in heaven. Give us this day our daily bread and forgive us our trespasses as we forgive those who trespass against us. And lead us not into temptation but deliver us from evil for thine is the kingdom and the power and glory forever. Amen.

Closing Song: "I'm Gonna Sing When The Spirit Says Sing"

*"The Friend Who Came at Midnight" from *20 Ways to Use Drama* by Judy Gattis Smith, published by Griggs Educational Service. Used with permission.

Followers of Jesus

Preparation for the Service

This children's liturgy attempts to introduce the children to the twelve disciples and to show how workers in the church today are also disciples.

To Prepare

1. Choose a child reader for scripture.

2. Choose twelve children to be the twelve disciples. They may be costumed. They will proceed down the aisle and make a few statements about themselves. Rehearse with them. You may need to make arrangements for amplifying their voices.

3. Choose a song leader to lead the group in singing "Disciple Song" to the tune of "Farmer In The Dell."

4. Rehearse with the children who will go into the audience and get local church leaders.

5. Have the children cut footsteps from colored construction paper to place in each seat.

Order of Service

Opening Remarks

Hymn: "O Young And Fearless Prophet"

Selecting the Twelve
 Scripture
 Song: "Fishers Of Men"
 Scripture
 Prayer

Meeting the Disciples

Procession of Twelve Disciples

Meeting Our Church Workers
(pass out list with order of names to be sung) (tune: "The Farmer In The Dell")

Song: "I Have Decided To Follow Jesus"

Dedication

Closing Hymn: "Living For Jesus"

Leader: Welcome to our children's liturgy. We have come together today in Jesus' name because we believe in him. Jesus showed us how to live as good people and he asked that others follow in his footsteps and try to live as he lived. Let us sing about this Jesus.

Hymn: "O Young And Fearless Prophet"

Leader: When Jesus lived there were a large number of people who followed him. This wide community that was attracted by his teaching and his leadership was called "the many." From this group he selected twelve special people to be his close disciples. Listen to the stories of how these special disciples were chosen.

Child Reader: Luke 5:1-11

Leader: Six of his twelve disciples were fishermen and Jesus said, "You will be fishers of men." You will bring others into the church and to Jesus' way of life.

Song: "Fishers Of Men"

Leader: Jesus called one disciple who was a tax collector.

Child Reader: Luke 5:27-28

Leader: Now Jesus had seven disciples. Do you know how he chose the other five?

Child Reader: Luke 6:12-13

Leader: Jesus spent all night praying before he chose the other disciples. Following his example, let us now pray.

Heavenly Father, help us, like Jesus, to come to you when we have a decision to make. Help us, like Jesus, to choose our friends carefully. Help us, like Jesus, to know we can talk everything over with you. Amen.

Meeting the Disciples

(Disciples proceed one at a time from the back of the room. They may be dressed in costumes of the period. The congregation sings the following words to the tune of "The Farmer In The Dell" as each enters. When a disciple reaches the front of the room, he introduces himself. Then the next disciple enters following the same format.)

Leader: Who were these twelve special disciples? Let's meet them now.

All sing: First there was Peter
First there was Peter
Hi Ho the Derry O
Come and follow me.

Peter: I am Peter. I was a simple fisherman who was sometimes weak and cowardly, but Jesus called me the "Rock" and the foundation of the Christian church.

All sing: Then there was Andrew
Then there was Andrew
Hi Ho the Derry O
Come and follow me.

Andrew: I am Andrew. I also was a fisherman, the brother of Peter. I was the first of the twelve to be called. I brought many people to Jesus. It was I who brought to Peter the boy with the loaves and the fishes.

All sing: Then there was James
Then there was James
Hi Ho the Derry O
Come and follow me.

James: I am James. I was Jesus' first cousin. Jesus nick-named me "Son of Thunder" because of my ambition and explosive temper.

All sing: Then there was John

Then there was John

Hi Ho the Derry O

Come and follow me.

John: I am John. I was the youngest of the disciples. I be-came known as the "disciple whom Jesus loved." I was the only disciple present at the crucifixion.

All sing: Then there was Philip

Then there was Philip

Hi Ho the Derry O

Come and follow me.

Philip: I am Philip. I was very sincere and practical. Some Greeks came to me and asked me to help them see Jesus.

All sing: Nathaniel-Bartholomew

Nathaniel-Bartholomew

Hi Ho the Derry O

Come and follow me.

Nathaniel-Bartholomew: I am Nathaniel-Bartholomew. I was the one who asked, "Can anything good come out of Nazareth?" But after meeting Jesus, I became an ardent dis-ciple.

All sing: Then there was Matthew

Then there was Matthew

Hi Ho the Derry O

Come and follow me.

Matthew: I am Matthew. I was a tax collector. I kept a care-ful and valuable record of Jesus' teaching.

All sing: There was James the Younger

There was James the Younger

Hi Ho the Derry O

Come and follow me.

James the Younger: I am James the Younger. I was the first bishop of Jerusalem and a pillar among Christians.

All sing: Then there was Judas

Then there was Judas

Hi Ho the Derry O

Come and follow me.

Judas: I am Judas, but not the man who betrayed Jesus. I was called Judas Thaddeaus. I served the master for three years and then I was Simon's companion on his missionary journeys.

All sing: Simon the Zealot

Simon the Zealot

Hi Ho the Derry O

Come and follow me.

Simon: I am Simon the Zealot. Before I followed Christ, I was a member of a radical group which used murder and sabotage to drive the Romans from the land. I gave this up to join Jesus.

All sing: Then there was Thomas

Then there was Thomas

Hi Ho the Derry O

Come and follow me.

Thomas: I am Thomas, the doubting disciple. But all my doubts dissolved in the presence of Jesus, my master.

All sing: Then there was Judas

Then there was Judas

Hi Ho the Derry O

Come and follow me.

Judas: I am Judas. I betrayed our Lord Jesus, but I thought I was acting for Jesus' own good.

Leader: There they are, the twelve whom Jesus called to be his special disciples. Wondering, exultant, full of praise and gratitude, they went with Jesus from place to place. They traveled with him along the seashore, over the mountains, into

the cities and villages. They saw his miracles. They heard his teaching and they grew in faith and understanding.
(*Disciples take seats in congregation*)

Leader: Now let us meet some of the disciples of this church. Some that Jesus has called to do his work.

First there's the preacher
First there's the preacher
Hi Ho the Derry O
Come and follow me.

(*Child goes into audience and gets minister [or ministers] and brings him/her forward*)

There are the musicians
There are the musicians
Hi Ho the Derry O
Come and follow me.

(*Child gets organist, choir director, singers, and so forth*)

There are the teachers
There are the teachers
Hi Ho the Derry O
Come and follow me.

(*Children go into audience and get church school teachers*)
(*Add to this list as fits your local congregation. After a group has gathered at the front, sing*):

We are all disciples
We are all disciples
Hi Ho the Derry O
Come and follow me.

Leader: We all want to say "thank you" to these special workers in our own church.

(*workers are seated*)

Leader: The last thing Jesus did was to reappear to his disciples with a promise.

Child Reader: Matthew 28:16-20

Leader: Let us now dedicate our lives to Jesus, who promised to be with us always, as our children sing, "I Have Decided To Follow Jesus."

Song: "I Have Decided To Follow Jesus"

Leader: Will each of you now take the paper footstep at your seat and write your name on it with the words: "I will follow Jesus"? The ushers will collect them and present them at the altar.

Closing Hymn: "Living For Jesus"

God Bless the Animals I Love (An Outdoor Service)

Preparation for the Service

Children seem to feel a special kinship with animals. Care of pets is often their first experience of loving responsibility. This liturgy seeks to affirm this experience in the Christian community.

To Prepare

1. Decide on a safe outside area for the service.
2. Send out announcements inviting all children to bring their pets, dogs on leashes and cats in carriers, to the service. Tell the children to dress informally.
3. Choose a leader for the whirling statue game and the storytelling.
4. The hymns suggested are available in most hymnals. Choose music that is appropriate for your audience. One church doing this service used "Old McDonald Had A Farm" substituting each child's name and sounds of his/her pet. For example: "Little Amy had a cat, Eee I, eee I O."

Order of Service

Gathering to Worship

Opening Remarks and Setting of Theme

Hymn: "This Is My Father's World"

Introduction of Pets and Owners

Poem: "God Bless The Animals I Love"

Prayers

Pastoral Prayer

Hymn: "All Things Bright And Beautiful"

Proclaiming Our Faith

Scripture

Sermon: "Whirling Statue of Animals"

Acts of Dedication / Pledge of Pet Owners

Closing Hymn: "All Things Bright And Beautiful"

Children bring their pets, on leashes or in carriers, to service.

Leader: Welcome adults! Welcome boys and girls! Welcome animals! We come together today to give thanks. We thank God enthusiastically for making his creation so wonderful. We are thankful for the sun, clouds, flowers, a juicy apple, and especially today for our pets. How much richer our lives are because of these furry friends, feathered friends, and swimming friends — all of our pets.

A famous poet said:
> *"He prayeth best who loveth best*
> *All creatures great and small*
> *For the dear God who loveth us*
> *He made and loveth all."*
> — Samuel Taylor Coleridge (public domain)

This is the theme of our service today: God who loves us, made and loves all his creatures.

Hymn: "This Is My Father's World"

We will ask our guests to tell us their names. Would those of you who have pets with you today please introduce them to us also?

Child Reader: Those of you who have brought pets and those of you who have come to our service today know what it means to love animals. You know the comfort and loyalty pets bring and you know the joy and richness wild creatures add to our world.

Jesus must have loved animals too. He spoke of finding lost sheep and how God watches over even the sparrows.

Leader: At this time in our service we usually offer our prayers to God. You know that sometimes we pray for ourselves and sometimes we pray for others. Today, using a prayer that comes from the Society for Prevention of Cruelty to Animals, we are going to pray on behalf of our animals. Let us pray:

We beseech thee, O Lord, to hear our supplication on behalf of the dumb creatures who, after their kind, bless, praise and magnify thee forever. Grant that all cruelty may cease out of our land and deepen our thankfulness to thee for the faithful companionship of those whom we delight to call our friends.

In silence let us ask God's forgiveness for the times we have been cruel to animals and for the times we have forgotten to feed or take care of our animals.

Help us, who are blessed with pets, to be kind and gentle and thoughtful toward all your creatures. Amen.

Hymn: "All Things Bright And Beautiful"

Proclaiming Our Faith

Child Reader: Genesis 1:26. Let them have dominion over the fish of the sea, the birds of the air and the cattle and over all the wild animals and all the creatures that crawl on the ground.

This passage tells the story of creation. It reminds us again of how God created all things, all creatures — great and small.

Leader: Animals are mentioned many times in the Bible. Did you know that? Today we are going to learn about some of these animals and we are going to do it by playing a game. How many of you know how to play the "whirling statue" game? Will three children please come forward for this game? I am going to swing each of you around then let you go gently so that you fall in just any random position. In whatever position you fall, you must "freeze" and hold that position. Then I will tell the audience which bird or animal I was thinking of, and the audience will decide which of you looks most like that animal.

(*whirl children*)

Leader: The first animal is a sheep. Which child looked most like a sheep to you?

(*choose child then all sit down*)

Leader: Do any of you know stories where sheep were mentioned in the Bible?

(*accepts answers from the group, they may mention flocks of Christmas sheep or others, acknowledge these*)

Jesus once told a story about a lost sheep. A good shepherd had 100 sheep. At the end of a long day of carefully caring for his sheep he was turning them into the fold for the night. He called each sheep and began counting them. One was missing! It was beginning to get dark, but instead of just saying, "Oh, I'll wait until morning," the good shepherd called another shepherd to watch over his flock and he set out to look for the little lost sheep. There are many things that can happen to a little sheep who has wandered away from the flock and from the good shepherd's care. There are poisonous plants that little sheep can eat. There are big eagles flying back and forth with watchful eyes looking for a stray lamb. There are dangerous passes where falling rocks can injure a sheep or where snakes lie in wait. The good shepherd looked and looked, though it was getting darker and colder.

What did it matter that he still had 99 sheep? What did it matter that a warm fire and tasty food were waiting for him back at the fold? One little lamb was lost, and that was all that mattered. Just as he was about to give up, the good shepherd heard a faint cry. The little lamb had missed his footing and fallen into a deep gorge. All night he had lain there in fear, hearing the cries and scratchings of wild animals nearby.

Slowly and carefully the good shepherd edged himself over the side until he could just reach one shivering little paw. Straining his tired muscles, the good shepherd slowly pulled the frightened lamb to safety. And then, what rejoicing! He lifted the weak little lamb onto his shoulder and ran home shouting: "The lost has been found."

Jesus told that story to show that God is like the good shepherd and we are like the lamb. When we are lost and frightened and alone, God is out there looking for us.

Let's have three more players now for another animal. (*choose three other children to play whirling statue*)

This time our animal is an eagle. Which child looked most like an eagle?

(*audience chooses then children sit down*)

In our last story the eagle was the bad guy looking for the little lost lamb. But there is another verse in the Bible about an eagle. Do you know what eagles look like? What color are they? Are they strong or weak birds?

Once a long time ago, the children of Israel were wandering for many years in the desert. Their great leader, Moses, had led them out of Egypt where they had been slaves; but before they could reach home, the Promised Land, they had many years of wandering back and forth. They were always in fear that the Egyptians might capture them again and take them back as slaves, and they were just plain tired of putting up tents, staying a while, then moving on. They were tired of sand in their eyes and the constant burning rays of the sun.

But then they would look up and see a mighty eagle soaring over their heads and it would give them encouragement. There are verses in the Bible, in the Old Testament, from Isaiah 40:28-31 that say: "Have you not known? Have you not heard? The Lord is the everlasting God, the Creator of the ends of the earth. He does not faint or grow weary; his understanding is unsearchable. He gives power to the faint, and strengthens the powerless. Even youths will faint and be weary, and the young will fall exhausted; but those who wait for the Lord shall renew their strength, they shall mount up with wings like eagles, they shall run and not be weary, they shall walk and not faint."

Let's think about these words. God is always there when we need him. He does not go to sleep or get tired or just forget us. We all feel depressed and discouraged sometimes, but the energy of God can give us the strength of eagles.

Let's play one more game of whirling statue. Could I have three more children?

(*play game*)

This time our animal is a donkey. Which child looked most like a donkey?

(*audience chooses and the children sit down*)

How many of you know the story of Palm Sunday? What happened? Jesus rode into Jerusalem on a donkey while children and adults ran alongside him waving palm branches and shouting, "Hosannah! Blessed is he that comes in the name of the Lord." It was a parade of a king. Yet in Jesus' day a king would have ridden a horse, perhaps a solid white, high-stepping plume-decorated horse. But Jesus chose a simple, little donkey, the animal that the people rode. A donkey is a humble beast who, with his owner, bears the burden and heat of the day, and offers his simple life in service. This story helps remind us that even ordinary people, even children, can be used by God for his purpose.

Animals help us learn many things, and they are referred to many times in the Bible. Jesus used animals in many of his parables, and animals were present at his birth. Let's remember what we learned from the Bible and the animals the next time we feel discouraged or weary or lost or that God can't have much use for us. He is always present when we are lost or weary, and he has a special use for each of us, no matter how small we are.

Acts of Dedication

We have a responsibility to pets as well as the pleasure and knowledge we receive from them. Will all pet owners please stand? Will you dedicate yourself now to being a better pet owner? If you agree, will you say, "I will" to the questions I ask you?

Will you promise to always be kind and tender to your pets and all of God's creatures?
(*I will*)

Every creature needs a home, a hole in the ground or in a tree or some sort of shelter. Will you provide your pet with a clean home?
(*I will*)

All animals need fresh drinking water. Some creatures get trash and dirt in their drinking water. Will you provide your pet with clean, fresh water daily and with food?
(*I will*)

The less animals and birds are handled the better it is for them. Will you love your pets and stroke them, but be careful to handle them gently?
(*I will*)

O Master, Creator of the world, we ask your blessing on both man and beast. Amen.

Closing Hymn: "All Things Bright And Beautiful"

Is This the Road to Bethlehem?
(A Children's Liturgy for Advent)

Preparation for the Service

Christmas is one of the great festival times in the church year. This service attempts to show children that this event followed a period of long waiting: that Christmas was not just an event in Bethlehem, but was the culmination of a people's hope and dream.

This liturgy can be used as a four-week Advent study. See page 45 for the instructions.

To Prepare

1. Choose child leaders for responsive sentences and prayer.
2. Arrange with children's choir or church school class for special music.
3. Cut out wooden or stiff cardboard figures and stands for action/sermon. Have children paint them (see instructions page 44).
4. Choose children to take part in the action/sermon. Practice.
5. Check with the church school classes about the presentation of gifts. (pre-school children with mittens; elementary classes with Salvation Army stockings; older elementary, food) Perhaps you would prefer gifts and other recipients that are more appropriate to your church.
6. Practice with the acolytes for the ritual of lighting Advent candles.

There are many talented people in our churches who are willing, even anxious, to help but who would feel uncomfortable teaching or leading. Is there someone in your congregation who does woodworking, carving, or artwork? Ask this person to make the simple figures suggested in this liturgy. You will need six figures with stands for each child.

For these activities, you will need space as well as brushes for each child and a variety of paints.

Figures for "Is This the Road to Bethlehem?"

Cut from 1/2 inch plywood, six figures approximately 14 inches tall, or similar figures cut from sturdy cardboard.

Paint with a prime coat of white. Let dry. Draw features and paint robes with tempera or oil paints.

Cut piece of wood for stands. Groove each so that character's feet fit and they will stand.

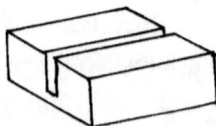

First Week of Advent

Give two figures to each child. Instruct them to paint their figures with a prime coat of white. Set them on their stands to dry. As the students are painting, or as their figures are drying, tell them about Abraham and Jacob. Use the material in this liturgy and supplement with stories about these two characters found in the Bible. Choose your favorite stories.

Second Week of Advent

The children can paint features and the robes of Abraham and Jacob. It would be helpful to have colorful Old Testament pictures for inspiration. The students also prime two more figures, Joseph and Moses, and hear stories about their lives.

Third Week of Advent

Two more figures are given to each child. These figures will represent David and Isaiah. After priming these two figures and hearing about their place on the road to Bethlehem, the children can put the finishing touches on all six of their figures. Make plans for a rehearsal and time to complete any painting.

Fourth Week of Advent

The children will perform the liturgy. Afterward they can take their figures home.

Order of Service

Prelude

Welcome

Procession of Acolytes

Opening Hymn: "O Come, Little Children"

Responsive Sentences

Prayer

Scripture

Children's Choir Anthem

Action/Sermon

Presentation of Gifts

Closing Hymn: "O Come, All Ye Faithful"

Prelude

Leader: Welcome to our children's liturgy. We come together today to think about and celebrate the birth of Jesus.

(*Acolytes enter down aisle as leader reads:*)
Leader: Men travel bravely by a thousand roads
   Some broad and lined with palaces
   Some hard and steep and lonely which blindly twist through tangled jungles where there is no light.
   And mostly they are traveled thoughtlessly;
   But once a year an ancient question comes to every traveler passing on the way.
   A question that can stab and burn, or bless,
   Is this the road that leads to Bethlehem?
— source unknown

Leader: Let the candles that light that path be lighted.

(*Acolytes light Advent candles*)

Opening Hymn: "O Come, Little Children"

Responsive Sentences

Child Leader: We come thankfully before you, O God;
Response: On the road to Bethlehem.
Child Leader: We join with the wise men who bring great gifts;
Response: On the road to Bethlehem.
Child Leader: We join lowly shepherds who hurry to the stable;
Response: On the road to Bethlehem.
Child Leader: We join with our family, our friends, and our church;
Response: On the road to Bethlehem.

Child Leader: Be with us and hear us and lead us, O God;
Response: On the road to Bethlehem.

Prayer (by child): Let us pray. As we make the journey to Bethlehem we confess we have not always done our best. We have put rocks and bumps in the road with our selfishness. We have not listened to God's word. We have not been as helpful to our parents and our teachers and our friends as we could be. We have not thought much about the sick and lonely people and tried to comfort them. We have wanted our own way a lot of the time. We are sorry for our selfishness and want to do better.

Leader: Boys and girls, God has wrapped his arms around you with his forgiveness. To thank him for his goodness and care for us, let us put our arms on each other's shoulders and pray the prayer he taught us to pray.

The Lord's Prayer (*unison*)

Leader: Let us listen now to the story of the first journey to Bethlehem. Listen carefully to the story, because I will ask you a question when it is finished.

Scripture: Luke 2:1-20

Leader: Who remembers what the shepherds said to one another when the angel went away? (*accept answers from the children*) "Let us go to Bethlehem and see this thing that has happened that the Lord has told us." Our children's choir will tell us more about this story.

Children's choir or church school class sings: "How Far Is It To Bethlehem?" or "How Many Miles To Bethlehem?" or "Shepherds, Shepherds, Where Are You Going?"

Action/Sermon

Leader: The road to Bethlehem is a long, long road. For many years people had waited for a Savior to be born. We think of Christmas as the story of the birth of Jesus, and it is; but another way to think of Christmas is to remember some of the Old Testament stories and events leading up to the birth of Christ. Let's remember now some of these people who traveled the long road to Bethlehem, waiting for a Savior.

(Setting: long table with manger at one end; children bring up wooden figures and line them up on the road to Bethlehem)

Congregation: one verse of "Come, Thou Long-Expected Jesus"

(Child 1 comes to the front carrying wooden figure s/he has painted. S/he holds it up for the congregation to see.)
Child 1: Here is Abraham, the great forefather of the Hebrew people. He is thought to have lived about 2000 BC. At the time of Abraham, most of the people of the world believed in many gods. Abraham came to believe that there was only one true God. One day he heard the voice of God telling him to leave his home in the Arabian desert and travel westward to the land known as Canaan to make a new home there. He took all his family and possessions and made the long, hard journey. He walked to the promised land. He was waiting for a Savior.
(places wooden figure on stand on the table and is seated)

Congregation: another verse of "Come, Thou Long-Expected Jesus"

(Child 2 brings up wooden figure that s/he has painted and holds it up for the congregation to see)

Child 2: Here is Jacob, the grandson of Abraham. Once Jacob had a fight with his brother and ran away from home. Jacob traveled over valleys and mountains and through forests and fields. One night he was very weary and lay down to sleep under the open sky. He dreamed that a great ladder of light rose from the earth, its top reaching to heaven. On the highest rung stood God, who renewed to Jacob the promise he had made to Abraham that the land of Canaan should belong to their descendants. After many years, Jacob decided to return home. On the way home God appeared to him and told him to change his name to Israel, and after that the Hebrews called themselves Israelites, or the children of Israel. Jacob was waiting for a Savior.
(places wooden figure on stand on the table and is seated)

(Child 3 brings up wooden figure that s/he has painted and holds it up for the congregation to see.)
Child 3: Here is Joseph, Jacob's favorite son. Because of jealousy, his brothers sold him into slavery and he was carried off into the land of Egypt. After many hardships he rose to a place of power in the Egyptian government. When a great famine hit the nation, Joseph forgave his brothers and brought them and his father and all of their families to live with him in Egypt. He spent his life trying to follow God, doing his best in a strange land, waiting for a Savior.
(places wooden figure on stand on the table and is seated)

Congregation: another verse of "Come Thou Long-Expected Jesus"

(Child 4 brings up wooden figure s/he has painted and holds it up for the congregation to see.)

Child 4: Here is Moses. For 400 years the children of Israel lived happily in Egypt. They prospered and increased, and then changes came about. A new pharaoh who hated the Hebrews and made them slaves, ruled over Egypt. The people suffered greatly. Moses led them out of Egypt into the wilderness. It was a hard life. They found no city to live in. They were hungry and thirsty and weary. But God was with them. In the desert he gave Moses the Ten Commandments and he always led them and fed them. For many years they wandered about seeking the holy land that God had promised them. Moses died on a lonely mountain before the people entered the promised land. Moses had been given the law, but he waited for truth and grace. He waited for a Savior.
(*places wooden figure on stand on the table and is seated*)

Congregation: another verse of "Come Thou Long-Expected Jesus"

(*Child 5 brings up wooden figure s/he has painted and holds it up for the congregation to see.*)
Child 5: Here is David. After the Hebrews had settled in Canaan he became their greatest king. He made Jerusalem the capital city. Here he brought the sacred chest containing the Ten Commandments. He built a tabernacle where it could be kept. David reigned for forty years, waiting for a Savior.
(*places wooden figure on stand on the table and is seated*)

Congregation: another verse of "Come Thou Long-Expected Jesus"

(*Child 6 brings up wooden figure s/he has painted and holds it up for the congregation to see.*)
Child 6: Sad to say, the kingdom built up to such magnificence by David and his son Solomon was not to last. Enemies destroyed the cities and captured the people. During

that time men of godly spirit arose who believed that they were directed by God to lead their people back to the ways of righteousness. These great religious leaders were called prophets. The noblest of the prophets was Isaiah. He was filled with a sense of the greatness of God. He dreamed of a golden age when the ways of men would be the ways God had taught them, and all injustice and wrong would be swept away. He dreamed and taught and preached, waiting for a Savior.
(places wooden figure on stand on the table and is seated)

Leader: And the wonderful news we have to tell is that in the fullness of time, God did send a Savior; a child was born in Bethlehem who would show the world how to live. He would show them what God was really like. He would be like a light shining through the many years of dark waiting. It was as Isaiah had prophesied.

Child 6: "The people who walked in darkness have seen a great light; those who lived in a land of deep darkness — on them the light has shined... For a child has been born for us, a son given to us; authority rests upon his shoulders; and he is named Wonderful Counselor, Mighty God, Everlasting Father, Prince of Peace" (Isaiah 9:2, 6).

Gifts of the Children
Leader: The people who first came to the manger at Bethlehem brought gifts. The wise men brought gold and frankincense and myrrh. The shepherds brought lambs and piped a merry tune for the new baby. If we came to the manger, we might bring clothes to keep the baby warm. Since we can't go to Bethlehem, we can share those gifts with children here.
(pre-school children bring forward mittens to be given to a local day care center)

If we came to the manger, we might bring toys. Since we can't go to Bethlehem, we can share those gifts with children here.
(*elementary children bring forward Salvation Army stockings which they have filled*)

If we came to the manger, we might bring food. Since we can't go to Bethlehem, we can share those gifts with children here.
(*older elementary children bring forward canned goods*)

Accept these gifts, O Father. We bring them to Bethlehem remembering your words: "Inasmuch as you have done it unto one of the least of these, you have done it unto me."

Closing Hymn: "O Come, All Ye Faithful"

Let's Celebrate Laughter!

Preparation for Service

This liturgy is ideal for a church with a clown ministry but it isn't mandatory. There are other churches with a clown ministry that may be available to participate. Pictures of the three types of clowns (whiteface, august, acrobat) can be substituted.

1. Choose clowns and arrange for their props.
2. Practice the game "laughing handkerchief."
3. Choose characters for sermon/skit. You will need these actors:

    clown
    two boys
    fat man
    professor
    sour-faced lady
    young girl

4. Purchase clown face make-up or face painting crayons (optional).

Order of Service

Opening Remarks and Setting of Theme

Song: "Joy, Joy, Joy, Joy Down In My Heart"

Laughing Handkerchief Game

Story of Sarah and Isaac

Song: "If You're Happy And You Know It, Clap Your Hands"

Prayer Meditation with Clowns

Sermon/Play: "The Clown Who Forgot How to Laugh"

Benediction with Clown Paint

Closing Hymn: "Joy To The World, The Lord Is Come" or "This Is The Day"

There's nothing worth the wear of winning
But laughter and the love of friends
— Belloc

Leader: Welcome to our children's liturgy.

Many times our church services help us consider serious and solemn subjects. Many times our church services have periods of silence where we sit and listen for God's word. Many times we use our best formal manners to show our great respect for God. But our God is the God of all creation. He has given us *many* wonderful gifts and we rejoice in them all. Today we come together to celebrate the gift of laughter and joy. Make a joyful noise unto the Lord all ye lands. Service the Lord with gladness. Come before his presence with singing.

Song: "Joy, Joy, Joy, Joy Down In My Heart"

Leader: Laughter is a wonderful gift from God and it seems that children have an especially abundant supply of this gift. Children seem to understand, better than we adults, that work, though necessary and good, is not the end of life. God puts us in his world to sometimes just laugh and enjoy. Sometimes God says to us "Wait a minute! This is not a grim, dull, motionless world. I have created a world of hope and joy, a world in which the unexpected can happen, a world of laughter."

Have all of you here had a good laugh today? If you haven't, maybe your laugh machine is rusty from lack of use. We'd better oil it. Here is a laughing handkerchief. I am going to toss it in the air. As soon as it leaves my hand everyone here must start laughing. But the minute the handkerchief touches the floor, everyone must stop immediately. There must be complete silence.

(This is usually a hilarious game in which at least one of your gigglers will not be able to stop laughing at the correct time. Play the game a number of times with comments

like: "That was pretty good but let's laugh a little harder." At first the laughter is forced, but about the third time it should be genuine. When the congregation seems relaxed, stop the game. Three or four times will probably do it.)

Leader: That's much better. Now we shouldn't have any more trouble laughing today. You know, boys and girls, the people in the Bible had the same feelings we do; that's one thing that makes it such a great book. There is a story in the Bible about a woman who had a good laugh. The woman's name was Sarah. Her husband was Abraham. God had chosen Abraham to be the leader of his people and Abraham had promised always to follow God. God had told Abraham that his descendants would be past all counting. There would be children and children's children and children's children's children. But the years passed and Abraham and Sarah grew old and they had no children.

"Perhaps I misunderstood God," Abraham finally decided and they grew older still.

One day Abraham was sitting in front of his tent when he saw three strangers coming toward him. Abraham was a friendly man so he invited them in to rest in the shade and have some food. It turned out these were no ordinary men, but heavenly visitors. While they were eating, one of the visitors asked, "Abraham, where is your wife Sarah?" Abraham answered, "She is in her tent."

"Next year at this time," the stranger said, "she will have a son."

The walls of a tent are very thin and this stranger had a loud booming voice so Sarah overheard everything he was saying. She got tickled. Here she was, an old lady with gray hair and failing eyesight. How could *she* have a baby? The more she thought about it the more she laughed. She laughed so loud that Abraham heard her, but he pretended not to because he didn't want to hurt the stranger's feelings.

But do you know the visitors were right and a year later Abraham and Sarah had a son. The Bible says Abraham was 100 years old. Sarah cried out, "God has given me a reason to laugh with joy." And they named that precious son Isaac, which means laughter.

Sarah recognized that nothing is too difficult with God, that she lived in a world where the unexpected did happen — a world of laughter.

We live in that kind of world too.

Song: "If You're Happy And You Know It, Clap Your Hands"

Leader: One of the characters that we associate with laughter is a clown. When we laugh at clowns we are really laughing at ourselves and that is good. We shouldn't always take ourselves *so* seriously. We are going to use clowns today to help us focus our prayer time.

There are three kinds of clowns. There are whiteface clowns.

(*one or more clowns enter in whiteface, wearing sad expressions, torn clothing*)

These poor clowns always look as if they are about to cry. Nothing they do seems to work out. Everything is always going wrong for them.

(*Clowns do a few simple routines. For example, one picks up a chair and it falls to pieces. He finally sits down and gets stuck in the seat.*)

Unison Prayer

Heavenly Father, we are all sad-faced clowns at times. Help us to see the funny side when everything goes wrong and help us never to forget that your world is a world of hope and joy. Amen.

Leader: There are also august clowns.

(*The clowns enter. They are slapstick clowns. They wear pants that fall down, noses that light up, and huge shoes they trip over. These clowns do a few routines.*)

Leader: We laugh at these clowns because what happens to them is so unexpected — like what happened to Sarah.

Unison Prayer

Heavenly Father, help us always to be aware that we live in a world where the unexpected can happen. Keep us open to the joy this belief brings. Amen.

Leader: And there are acrobat clowns.

(*There clowns enter. They turn summersaults, cartwheels, ride unicycles, and walk on stilts. They perform a few routines.*)

Unison Prayer

Heavenly Father, these clowns remind us that life is full of new possibilities, new ways of doing things. Keep us open to new awareness you have planned for us in this world of surprise and delight. Amen.

Leader: Our sermon today is going to be a play. It is also about a clown. But the worst possible thing had happened to this little clown. Ladies and gentlemen meet "The Clown Who Forgot How to Laugh."

(*Little clown enters, sits down sadly, his head in his hands.*)
(*Two boys enter, throwing a Frisbee®, laughing together.*)
Boy 1: Hey, look, there's a clown from the circus.
(*they walk over to the clown*)
Boy 2: Shouldn't you be inside? The performance has started in the big tent. All the clowns are there.

(*Clown shakes his head*)

Boy 1: What's the matter? Are you sick or something?

Boy 2: Yeah, why aren't you laughing and funny?

Clown: (*little clown lets out a big sob*) I can't laugh. I've forgotten how.

Boy 1: Forgotten? But people don't forget how to laugh.

Clown: Well, I did and (*between sobs*) the circus doesn't want me and (*sob*) I don't have a job — and…

Boy 2: Wait a minute, we'll help you.

Clown: You will?

Boy 2: Sure! Let's see now. We were laughing while we were trying to catch this Frisbee®. Here you go.

Clown: (*sails Frisbee® — tries a few throws*) It is no use. I can't laugh.

Boy 1: But it's so easy just to laugh.

Clown: Not for me — not anymore.

Boy 1: You know what I get tickled at — cartoons on TV. There's the (substitute children's favorites).

Clown: I've seen practically all the cartoons on TV — in living color, in black and white — first runs, reruns. It's no use.

Boy 2: Comic books and joke books — that's it! Boy, they really make me laugh.

Clown: It is no use I tell you. Books just aren't funny to me anymore.

Boy 1: You're a pretty silly clown. Come, we can't help him.

Boy 2: Yeah, I'm glad we can still laugh.

Clown: Oh my! Oh dear me! What will happen to me now? (*fat man comes along*)

Fat Man: What's the matter, little clown?

Clown: I can't laugh. I'm supposed to be funny and I can't even laugh.

Fat Man: You know what makes me feel jolly? Eating these funny cookies. (*pulls big sugar cookies from paper sack*)

The more I eat, the more I laugh. Here, try one.

Clown: Okay, maybe that will work. (*takes a bite*) No, I still feel sad (*sob*) — even sadder than before.

Fat Man: Well, I'm sorry but I'm afraid I can't help you.

(*Clown sobs loudly*)

(*lady wearing glasses and talking on smartphone enters*)

Lady: My dear little clown, whatever is the matter?

Clown: (*looks up*) Who are you?

Lady: I'm a professor at the university.

Clown: Oh, you are? Then maybe you can help me. You see I need to know how to laugh.

Lady: How to laugh — let me see, I think I have the information right here. (*looks at smartphone*) Yes here it is: Laugh: hearty laugh, giggle, laugh of scorn, titter. To laugh simply practice fifteen minutes a day. Go ahead now, try it. One, two, laugh.

Clown: (*Clown tries but sounds very artificial*) That's not laughing. I used to laugh and that's not laughing.

Lady: Hmph! This younger generation. They think they can just pick up something without even practicing.

(*she leaves*)

(*sour-faced lady enters*)

Sour-faced Lady: Well, now even the clowns aren't laughing these days.

Clown: I've forgotten how.

Sour-faced Lady: I'm not surprised. There's not much to laugh about these days. Violence — crime in the streets — it is a miserable world we live in. Keep up your gloom. If you feel bad you might as well tell the world.

Clown: I don't know. It seems as if the world is a nicer place if people smile.

Sour-faced Lady: The world's a rotten place! That's what I think.

(*sour-faced lady exits*)

(*a little girl enters*)

Girl: Oh, can you help me? I've lost my money. I've looked everywhere.

Clown: Sorry, I haven't seen it.

Girl: Oh no! It was my money for the circus. I won't get to see the clowns. It's too late now.

(*sits beside clown and cries*)

Clown: Wait a minute. I'm a clown. Stop crying and I'll show you what clowns do.

Girl: Will you? Will you really?

(*Clown does a few tricks. For example, he may run around child with bucket of water shouting "You're on fire! I'll save you!" After exaggerating the idea a few times he empties the bucket on her and it is full of confetti.*)

Girl: (*claps hands and laughs*) You're better than the whole circus. You are so funny!

Clown: I am?

Girl: Oh yes! I feel so much better now. I don't even care if I missed the circus.

Clown: You know something. As soon as I started trying to make you feel better, I started feeling good and I began chuckling. Hey! I remember how to laugh! I'll never forget how to laugh and be funny ever again. All you have to do is just try to make another person forget his troubles! This is great! Come on, maybe I can get my old job back now.

(*they exit*)

Leader: And it is just as ridiculous for us to forget how to laugh and rejoice in the Lord as it is for a circus clown. As we leave, let's all be clowns for just a moment and through a moment of fantasy experience with utmost abandon and joy the love of God.

(*Clowns spread through the congregation placing a dab of color from a make-up pot on the faces of the people — on the tip of the nose, cheek, or forehead — saying, "Go and rejoice in the Lord!")*

Closing Hymn: "Joy To The World, The Lord Is Come" or "This Is The Day"

Remember Your ABCs (Children's Celebration for the Beginning of School)

Preparation for the Service

The beginning of school is a special day in the lives of children. This liturgy seeks to capture the excitement of new beginnings both in school and Sunday school. To involve the whole congregation, do the opening procession in the sanctuary during a regular worship service if possible. Then the children may slip off their sandwich boards and join their parents for the remainder of the service or exit to a Sunday school room for a study session on Jesus as a young boy.

To Prepare

1. Make 26 sandwich-board signs. You will need two pieces of poster board for each sign and yarn to connect the two pieces so that they will fit over a child's head. On the back and front of each sign is a large alphabet letter.

2. Choose 26 children* for the opening procession. They will wear simple robes and the alphabet sign. Each will recite a verse from the book of Proverbs.

3. Rehearse this procession and recitation in the sanctuary at least once, striving for a feeling of dignity and drama. You may need to make arrangements for amplifying the children's voices. Practice the song "B-I-B-L-E."

4. Choose a child to bring in the Bible. Practice.

5. If the children exit for Sunday school lessons, you will need a picture of Jesus in a synagogue school. If you do not have one in your Sunday school files, find one in a web search online.

*If 26 children are not available, consider putting a different letter on the back of each board, so that 13 children can be in the procession.

Children wear simple choir or acolyte robes. Over this is worn two pieces of poster board like a sandwich board connected over the shoulders with yarn. An alphabet letter is painted on the front and back.

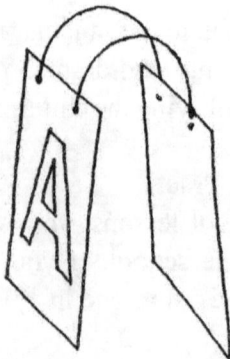

Order of Service

Opening Remarks

Procession of Bible

Hymn: "God Of Grace And God Of Glory"

Procession of Children

Reading of Proverbs

Prayer

Song: "B-I-B-L-E"

Responsive Sentences

Feedback Talk (in Sunday school class or sermon)

Benediction: Psalm 139

Closing Hymn: "Guide Me, O Thou Great Jehovah"

Leader: Welcome to our children's liturgy. Boys and girls, our summer vacation is over. It is time for the beginning of school again. You will be getting many new books at school this year — books that teach you about science and math and history. Each class and subject has a special book. In the church, we have a special book. Will you all stand as our Bible is brought to the altar?

(*procession of Bible*)
Hymn: "God Of Grace And God Of Glory"

Leader: Our Bible is a combination of many books. In the Bible are stories of history, literature, and poetry. There is also a book of wisdom in the Bible. It is called Proverbs. This book deals with common problems of everyday living. It deals with common sense and good manners. As we begin a new school year, we want to study this book and see what it says to each of us.

(*Twenty-six [or thirteen] alphabet children enter single file. They proceed in and circle the congregation. Organist plays "God Of Grace." When children have circled congregation, they come to the front.*)
Leader: In the book of Proverbs are many short sayings that give advice about how to be wise. We can find everything from A to Z. Let's listen now as we go through the alphabet, hearing advice from Proverbs.

"A" Child: (comes to pulpit or chancel and recites) A — Avoid evil and walk straight ahead. Don't go one step off the right way (Proverbs 4:27).
"B" Child: (comes to pulpit and "A" Child returns to seat) B — Be generous and you will be prosperous. Help others and they will help you (Proverbs 11:25).

"C" Child: (follows same pattern) C — Correction and discipline are good for children. If a child has his own way, he will make his mother ashamed of him (Proverbs 29:15).

"D" Child: D — Don't make friends with people who have hot, violent tempers. You might learn their habits and not be able to change (Proverbs 22:24-25).

"E" Child: E — Enthusiasm without knowledge is not good; impatience will get you into trouble (Proverbs 19:2).

"F" Child: F — Friends always show their love. What are brothers for, if not to share trouble? (Proverbs 17:17).

"G" Child: G — God keeps every promise he makes. He is like a shield for all who seek his protection (Proverbs 30:5).

"H" Child: H — Hot tempers cause arguments, but patience brings peace (Proverbs 15:18).

"I" Child: I — If you refuse to learn you are hurting yourself. If you accept correction you will become wiser (Proverbs 15:32).

"J" Child: J — Joy is to find just the right word for the right occasion! (Proverbs 15:23).

"K" Child: K — Kind words bring life, but cruel words crush a man's spirit (Proverbs 15:4).

"L" Child: L — Let other people praise you — even strangers; never do it yourself (Proverbs 27:2).

"M" Child: M — Men may make their plans, but God has the last word (Proverbs 16:1).

"N" Child: N — Never say something that isn't true. Have nothing to do with lies and misleading words (Proverbs 4:24).

"O" Child: O — Old men are proud of their grandchildren, just as boys are proud of their fathers (Proverbs 17:6).

"P" Child: P — Pay attention to your teacher and learn all you can (Proverbs 23:12).

"Q" Child: Q — A quote from King Solomon: "Being wise is better than being strong."

"R" Child: R — Refuse good advice and you are asking for trouble; follow it and you are safe (Proverbs 13:13).

"S" Child: S — Sometimes it takes a painful experience to make us change our ways (Proverbs 20:30).

"T" Child: T — Too much honey is bad for you, and so is trying to win too much praise (Proverbs 25:27).

"U" Child: U — Unreliable messengers cause trouble, but those who can be trusted make peace (Proverbs 13:17).

"V" Child: V — Virtue is to look beyond it when someone wrongs you (Proverbs 19:11).

"W" Child: W — When you please the Lord, you can make your enemies into friends (Proverbs 16:7).

"X" Child: X — Read your book of Proverbs and put an "X" beside every proverb that you need to work on.

"Y" Child: Y — You do yourself a favor when you are kind. If you are cruel, you only hurt yourself (Proverbs 11:17).

"Z" Child: Z — Zero in on all this good advice.

Leader: Let us pray. Heavenly Father, open our minds to all that you would teach us. Help us to take this advice from your book of wisdom. You have given us minds that can think and plan and understand and choose. Guide us into choosing your way for our lives. Help us to understand your great love and your great wisdom, power, and might. Open our hearts and minds to your words. Amen.

Song: "B-I-B-L-E" sung by children

From our New Testament we read about the life of Jesus. We don't know too much about his boyhood, but we find these words, "Jesus grew in wisdom and stature and favor with God and man." Let us read responsively:

All: Help us grow in wisdom and stature and favor with God and man.

Leader: As we study and prepare our lessons,

All: help us grow in wisdom and stature and favor with God and man.

Leader: As we play with our friends at recess and after school,

All: help us grow in wisdom and stature and favor with God and man.

Leader: As we cooperate with our teachers,

All: help us grow in wisdom and stature and favor with God and man.

Children exit to classrooms for study about Jesus as a boy.

(sermon by minister may be substituted here)

Leader: When Jesus was a boy he went to school, but if you had gone with him you would have found many things about it very strange to you. *(show picture)*

First, notice what the school itself looked like. What are some of the things that are different?

(accept suggestions from the children)

Leader might add: The students sat on mats upon stone or tile floors and some classes were held outside. There were no desks, not even chairs. Instead of a separate school building, the students met in the local synagogue.

What do you notice about the teacher? Who do you think he was?

(accept answers)

The rabbi of the synagogue was the teacher. When a boy was six or seven years of age, his father and the local rabbi began guiding his instruction. What kinds of supplies did they use?

(accept answers)

There were no books as we have them, but the rabbi read from scrolls and the students used clay tablets to practice their writing. Often they recited their lessons out loud, all at the same time.

What do you notice about the way the students are dressed?

(*accept answers*)

The students wore small caps. We consider it rude to keep your hat on inside the church. However, these students were taught that covering their heads showed respect and reverence to God.

Does anyone notice anything else about the students?

(*accept answers*)

There were no girls present in the classroom. Only Jewish boys were educated at the synagogue school.

What kind of a student do you think Jesus would have been? Why?

(*accept answers*)

When Jesus grew to be a man he told people how God wanted them to live. What do you think he would have told you about being a student at school this year?

(*accept answers*)

The psalms that we love from our Bible are the same ones that Jesus learned. For our benediction let's read aloud together from Psalm 139 as the students in Jesus' day did.

(*put words on overhead projector or on a sign*)

Search me, O God and know my heart.
Try me and know my thoughts.
And see if there be any wicked way in me
And lead me in the way everlasting.

Closing Hymn: "Guide Me, O Thou Great Jehovah"

Sidewalk Celebration
(An Outdoor Service)

Preparation for the Service

The stories and teachings of Jesus take on new meaning for children as they see them expressed visually and as they themselves help in the creation. This service is to be held in a large, concrete parking lot or on a large sidewalk.

To Prepare

1. Choose six adult leaders to tell teachings of Jesus and supervise drawings.
2. Decide on the place for the service, either a sidewalk or a parking lot. Divide your space into six large sections not too close together.
3. Assemble a complete set of sidewalk chalk for each square.

Order of Service

Welcome / Gathering

Hymn: "Tell Me The Stories Of Jesus"

Dispersion and Creation of Chalk Pictures

Regathering Time

Seeing and Hearing the Stories Created by the Groups

Leader: Hello! Welcome to our children's liturgy. We are here today for a sidewalk celebration. The things that stand out in Christian worship are our devotion to Christ, his person, his life; his teachings are our inspiration. Through the Bible we learn about the life he lived. We enter the world of Galilee, the lakeside, the hilltop. We walk with him along dusty trails and grassy slopes. Jesus told many stories during his life, and we want to remember and learn from these stories.

Hymn: "Tell Me The Stories Of Jesus"

Leader: Today for our worship we are going to hear again the teachings of Jesus. We will divide into six groups by counting off one to six. Each number has a corresponding number on one of the large squares on the sidewalk (or in the parking lot). In just a moment you will go to your correct square. When you get there a leader will tell you one of the teachings of Jesus, and then your whole group will illustrate it with chalk in your square on the sidewalk (or parking lot). When we have all finished we will gather again here and then we will form a procession and visit all of the squares, seeing and hearing again the wonderful stories of Jesus.
(*Children go to groups. Group leader reads the Bible story and the group talks about what it means and how they will illustrate it.*)

Square 1: The Sower

A man went out to sow. As he scattered the seed in the field, some of it fell along the path and birds came and ate it up. Some of it fell on rocky ground where there is little soil. The seeds soon sprouted because the soil wasn't deep. Then when the sun came up it burned the young plants and because the roots had not grown enough, the plants soon dried up. Some of the seed fell among thorns which grew up and choked the plants and they didn't bear grain. But some seeds fell in good soil and the plants sprouted, grew, and bore grain; some had thirty grains, others sixty, and others one hundred (Mark 4:3-8).

Square 2: The Two House Builders

A wise man built his house on a rock. The rain poured down, the rivers flooded over, and the winds blew hard against the house. But it did not fall, because it had been built on the rocks. But everyone who hears these words of mine and does not obey them will be like a foolish man who built his house on the sand. The rain poured down, the rivers flooded over, the winds blew hard against that house until it fell. What a terrible fall that was! (Matthew 7:24-27).

Square 3: Mustard Seed

The kingdom of God is like a mustard seed, the smallest seed in the world. A man takes it and plants it in the ground. After a while it grows up and becomes the biggest of all plants. It puts out such large branches that the birds come and make their nests in its shade (Mark 4:31-32).

Square 4: A Tree and Its Fruit

A healthy tree does not bear bad fruit, nor does a poor tree bear good fruit. Every tree is known by the fruit it bears. You do not pick figs from thorn bushes or gather grapes from bramble bushes. A good man brings good out of the treasure of good things in his heart; a bad man brings bad out of his treasure of bad things. For a man's mouth speaks what his heart is full of (Luke 6:43-45).

Square 5: Light of the World

You are like light for the whole world. A city built on a hill cannot be hid. Nobody lights a lamp to put it under a bowl. Instead, he puts it on the lampstand where it gives light for everyone in the house. In the same way your light must shine before people, so that they will see the good things you do and give praise to your Father in heaven (Matthew 5:14-16).

Square 6: Lilies of the Field

Do not be worried about the food and drink you need to stay alive or about the clothes for your body. After all, isn't life worth more than food? And isn't the body worth more than clothes? Look at the birds flying around. They do not plant seeds, gather a harvest, and put it in barns. Your Father in heaven takes care of them. And why worry about clothes? Look how the wild flowers grow. They do not work or make clothes for themselves. But I tell you that not even Solomon, as rich as he was, had clothes as beautiful as one of these flowers (Luke 12:22-28).

Regathering Time

Leader: Let's all form a single file line holding hands and we will visit squares and hear the teachings of Jesus.

Group sings one verse of "Tell Me The Stories Of Jesus" as they walk to the first square. They form a circle around the picture. Leader tells the story and explains the meaning and the illustration.

Leader: (*leads in prayer following this*) Father, we thank you for this story of Jesus. Give us ears to hear and hearts to understand its meaning. Amen.

Continue to do this for all six squares.

The Peaceable Kingdom

Preparation for the Service
In a world of violence, children need to be reminded of the ancient dream of the peaceable kingdom.

To Prepare
1. Make box costumes for use in sermon/procession (see instructions). More elaborate costumes are available at costume or party stores or can be made or created from appropriate Halloween costumes and masks. There are resources available online.
2. Practice songs: "Let There Be Peace On Earth" and "I've Got Peace Like A River."
3. Choose a child reader for scripture.
4. Choose someone to do prayer/meditation with gloves. Practice with him/her. The prayer of Saint Francis may be done to music or read.
5. Rehearse the processional and recessional of the "Peaceable Kingdom." Children will need to practice in their box costumes at least once.

To Create Box Costumes
1. Use grocery boxes big enough for children to climb into.
2. Draw animal features on box: add tail or snout or whiskers if you like.
3. Add shoulder straps that are tied around a stick on the inside of the box so they don't pull through holes.
4. Get inside.

Order of Service

Setting Theme of Peace

Song: "Let There Be Peace On Earth"

Scripture

Responsive Sentences

Song: "I've Got Peace Like A River"

Musical Prayer Meditation with Gloves

Sermon/Processional: "The Peaceable Kingdom"

Song: "Let There Be Peace On Earth"

Our Pledge to Be Peacemakers This Week

Passing of the Peace

Leader: Welcome to our children's liturgy. Try to imagine a time when there is no war going on anywhere, in any corner of the world. Try to imagine a time when the people and the nations of the world know that *all* people are children of *one* great God. Try to imagine a time when there is no jealousy or bickering, when people love one another and work together to do the will of God. Try to imagine a time when there are no disagreements or quarrels, when families live in harmony and friends are happy together. People have always dreamed of such a time, of such a place, and called it the peaceable kingdom.

Is it just a dream? What does it mean when the gospel message proclaims "good tidings of peace"? We have come together today to consider these questions.

Opening Song: "Let There Be Peace On Earth"
Leader: Hear the words of scripture.
Child Reader: Blessed are the peacemakers, for they will be called the children of God (Matthew 5:9).

Leader: We want to think now about the times when peace didn't begin with us. Will you pray with me? We remember the times we have argued;
All: Father, forgive us.
Leader: We remember the times we lost our tempers;
All: Father, forgive us.
Leader: We remember the times we have hurt other people's feelings;
All: Father, forgive us.
Leader: We remember the times we were jealous of others;
All: Father, forgive us.
Leader: We remember our fusses and fights;
All: Father, forgive us.
Leader: God does forgive us. Even better, he forgets and wipes all our mistakes away. All he asks is that we really try

to do better, to control our tempers, to think of others rather than ourselves. Then he gives us a promise about peace.

Child Reader: John 14:27: My peace I give to you.
Ephesians 2:14: For he is our peace.

Song: "I've Got Peace Like A River"

Meditation with Gloves

The prayer of Saint Francis may be read or sung to music.
(*Two hands in gloves appear above a stage or screen.*)
Reader: Lord, make me an instrument of thy peace. Where there is hatred —
(*hands clutched in fists*)
Let me show love,
(*hands open, palms up, receiving*)
Where there is injury,
(*right hand falls limply*)
Pardon,
(*left hand pats right hand in comfort*)
Where there is doubt —
(*hands rotate back and forth from wrist*)
Faith.
(*hands clasp each other in handshake*)
Where there is despair —
(*right hand in fist*)
Hope.
(*left hand goes to fist and uncurls the fingers very slowly*)
Where there is darkness —
(*hands walk in opposite directions*)
Light.
(*hands move slowly together until they touch palm to palm*)
Where there is sadness —
(*hands hang limply forward*)
Joy.
(*both hands up, wiggle all fingers very fast*)

Leader: The great prophet Isaiah told of the time of the coming Messiah. He spoke of what a truly peaceable kingdom would be like. Listen to what he said: "The wolf shall live with the lamb, the leopard shall lie down with the kid, the calf and the lion and the fatling together, and a little child shall lead them. The cow and the bear shall graze, their young shall lie down together; and the lion shall eat straw like the ox. The nursing child shall play over the hole of the asp, and the weaned child shall put his hand on the adder's den. They will not hurt or destroy on all my holy mountain; for the earth will be full of the knowledge of the Lord as the waters cover the sea" (Isaiah 11:6-9). To fully appreciate these verses, let's meet some of the animals and learn how they were regarded in those days. First, the bad guys.
The wolf —

(*wolf enters, walks down aisle to front of church*)

The wolf is mentioned numerous times in the Bible. It is almost always a symbol of treachery and ferocity. Genesis 49:27: "Benjamin is a ravenous wolf, in the morning devouring the prey, and at evening dividing the spoil."
The leopard —

(*leopard enters and comes to front*)

The leopard is mentioned several times in the Bible. He was feared because of his terrible strength. Jeremiah 5:6: "A leopard is watching against their cities; everyone who goes out of them shall be torn in pieces."
The bear —

(*bear enters and comes to front*)

The bear, mentioned in the Bible, was a menace to vineyard and to sheep and goats. It was regarded as second in fierceness only to the lion. We read of David saving his sheep from the ferocious bear.
The lion —

(*lion enters and comes to front*)

The lion is described in the Bible as the most powerful, daring, and impressive of all carnivores, and as having a terrifying roar. Amos 3:8: "The lion has roared; who will not fear?"

Even the cubs were to be feared —

(*cub enters and joins others*)

Isaiah 5:29: "Their roaring is like a lion, like young lions they roar; they growl and seize their prey, they carry it off, and no one can rescue."

Meet the asp —

(*asp enters and comes to front*)

There are more than twenty references to snakes in the Bible. The asp is a cobra. The ribs of the neck spread out to form a wide hood which it used to threaten enemies.

The cockatrice —

(*cockatrice enters*)

The cockatrice is a viper and is the only deadly snake north of the desert in Israel.

This is a pretty deadly group of characters, isn't it? Now Isaiah said that right alongside these would dwell the innocent, unprotected animals.

The lamb —

(*lamb enters and comes to front*)

And the kid —

(*kid enters and comes to front*)

Lambs are baby sheep and kids are baby goats. These were the two most important domesticated animals of the Hebrews and they were recognized as being gentle, helpless, and defenseless.

A cow and a calf —

(*cow and calf enter*)

A cow and a calf were also part of the domestic life of the Hebrews. Though they are larger than sheep and goats, they are also defenseless and very gentle.

An ox —
(*ox enters*)
Oxen were used in farm work. Sometimes they were stall-fed and very gentle. They were slow, dependable animals, sometimes used as beasts of burden.
And three little children —
(*children enter*)
Can you imagine these animals living peaceably together? Let's listen to the Bible verses again:
"The wolf shall dwell with the lamb."
(*wolf and lamb join hands*)
"The leopard shall lie down with the kid."
(*leopard and kid join hands*)
"The calf and the lion together."
(*calf and lion join hands*)
"And a little child shall lead them."
(*one of the children leads these animals out*)
"The cow and the bear shall feed."
(*cow and bear join hands*)
"And the lion shall eat straw with the ox."
(*cub and ox join hands*)
"The youngest child shall play over the hole of the asp."
(*asp and child join hands*)
"And the child shall put his hand on the adder's den."
(*child and adder join hands*)
"They shall not hurt nor destroy in all my holy mountain."
(*these animals leave*)
"The earth shall be full of the knowledge of the Lord as the waters cover the sea."

Leader: Now let's expand our thinking. Think of people who are supposed enemies getting along together.
(*congregation sits in silence*)

Think of a world where so-called enemy nations live in peace.

(*congregation sits in silence*)

Think of a world where no one would hurt or destroy.
(*congregation sits in silence*)

And remember the Bible says, "They shall not hurt nor destroy because the earth shall be full of the knowledge of God." Lord make us full of your knowledge so that we will not hurt nor destroy. Amen.

Song: "Let There Be Peace On Earth"

Leader: Father, press us until we long for peace and until we are willing to pursue it. Will all of you who are willing to dedicate yourselves as peacemakers this week raise your hands? This then is our pledge to God to be peacemakers this week.

For the benediction we will pass the peace. Cover the hands of the person next to you with your hands and say, "Peace of God be with you."

The Stone Is Rolled Away

Preparation for the Service

Death is a subject that children wonder about. This service seeks to explore the subject triumphantly in the context of the Christian community.

Someone skilled in paper arts and crafts would be helpful for this liturgy as three paper projects are suggested: a mural, scissor art, and an accordion picture.

To Prepare

1. Use a large piece of butcher paper. Mark five sections on the paper.

2. Divide the children into five groups. Each child then draws a picture illustrating the verse (or verses) he or she is given from Luke 24:1-12. Allow the child to do his/her own thing with crayons or markers. Some pictures may be cartoon-like, others realistic.

3. These pictures are glued into the appropriate section on the mural paper. Arrange the pictures collage style. You may have to cut some to fit within the proper space. Children's work is most attractive collectively. The impact of displaying pictures together heightens the effect of the biblical verse.

4. During the liturgy intersperse each section with the reading of scripture and song.

Preparation for Symbols of Easter

Someone skilled in the German scissor art of Scherenschnitte would be most effective here, however, a cricket craft cutter would also work. However if you do not have anyone skilled in paper-cutting you may use actual objects or pictures. You will need: an Easter egg, an Easter lily, a butterfly, and a sun.

Accordion Picture

1. Write on four poster boards the appropriate words found in the liturgy.

2. Tape the four pieces together so that they can be unfolded one at a time accordion-like.

A musician would also be helpful for this liturgy:

* to teach the song "The Stone Is Rolled Away" and lead it at the appropriate times during the scripture reading.

* to provide small bells for the children. During the closing hymn, "Christ The Lord Is Risen Today" children shake the bells on "Alleluia."

Order of Service

Opening Hymn: "Welcome Happy Morning"

Opening Remarks and Setting of Theme

Scripture Reading

Story: "Jesus Lives!"

Hymn: "He Lives!"

Responsive Prayer

Bible Reading with Mural and Song: "The Stone Is Rolled Away"

Cut Paper Symbols of Easter

God's Message about Death

Closing Hymn: "Christ The Lord Is Risen Today" (with bells)

Leader: Welcome to our children's liturgy. Today we will be talking about death. We have all heard about death, and sometimes we worry about it. Some of our pets have died and some of our grandparents. Some people die of old age and some die in accidents. All of us will die one day. Sometimes when we think of death (especially our own death) we are afraid. But let me ask you a question: Would you be afraid to go alone into the woods in the middle of the night? We would, wouldn't we? *But* would you be afraid if your parent went with you? No. We feel the same about death. We know that God cares for us and will be with us. Because we trust him, we are not afraid to die. Let's hear the familiar words of Psalm 23.

Child Reader: "The Lord is my shepherd, I shall not want. He makes me lie down in green pastures. He leads me beside still waters. He restores my soul. He leads me in paths of righteousness for his name's sake. Even though I walk through the valley of the shadow of death, I fear no evil. For thou art with me; thy rod and thy staff they comfort me."
I will give thanks to you, O God, for you comfort me.
I will trust and not be afraid, for God is my strength.

Leader: As Christians, we can be more than just unafraid of death. Because of Jesus, we can feel victorious about it. To understand this, let's hear again the story of Jesus' life.

Jesus Lives!
A long, long time ago, Jesus lived in the village of Nazareth. When he was a boy, he played with his friends. He helped his father in the carpenter shop. He grew tall and strong. He grew wise and kind. He grew to love people and God.

When Jesus became a man, he traveled about the country. He acted the way God wants people to act. He was kind and helpful to all sorts of people — the rich and the poor, the happy and the sad, the good and the bad. But he did what he knew was right, no matter what people said or thought.

He spoke the way God wants people to speak. He spoke the truth, no matter what happened to him.

"Love your enemies," he said. "Do good to those who do evil to you." "You make the temple a place for cheating and selling. It should be a house of prayer."

"All men are brothers. Have we not all one Father — God?"

"God loves and cares for each one of you."

Some people who saw and heard Jesus said, "I do not understand his strange ideas. Whoever heard of loving your enemy?"

Some said, "He is not a teacher from God. He's a dangerous person."

But some people who heard and saw Jesus said, "Surely, he is a special leader from God. He speaks the truth. I want to follow him."

As time went on, the enemies of Jesus had him arrested and brought to trial before the governor. The governor thought Jesus was innocent, but Jesus' enemies had said many evil things about him. They got other people to feel angry at Jesus too.

After Pilate the governor had questioned Jesus he said, "I can find no wrong in this man. What do you want me to do with him?"

The people shouted, "Kill him! Crucify him!"

Jesus was killed in the same way as criminals were killed at that time. Before he died, Jesus prayed to God, saying, "Father, forgive them; for they know not what they do." One of the soldiers who had helped with the crucifixion and was there to see how bravely Jesus died, said, "This surely was the Son of God."

After Jesus died, his friends were very sad. They went back to their homes and to their work. Soon something wonderful happened. They were no longer sad. "Jesus is not dead," they said. "He lives! He lives!"

Some of Jesus' friends were sure they saw him, the brightness in his eyes and the smile on his face. Some said that the grave where he was buried was empty. They all said that they knew Jesus was with them. They had been sad; now they were glad. They had been afraid; now they were strong and brave. They had hated the people who killed Jesus; now they loved and forgave them.

"He lives! He lives!" they said. "Surely this is God's doing!" They began to tell others about Jesus. Many people said, "We too know that Jesus is with us. We want to follow him."

And that is what we say today. "We know he is with us. We want to follow him."

Hymn: "He Lives!"

Responsive Prayer

Leader: Jesus loved people who were mean to him.
All: Help us to be like Jesus.
Leader: Jesus didn't worry about getting even with people.
All: Help us to be like Jesus.
Leader: Jesus was friendly to people others didn't like.
All: Help us to be like Jesus.
Leader: Jesus did things for others instead of himself.
All: Help us to be like Jesus.

Leader: We read from the Bible the story of Easter morning when friends of Jesus hurried to his tomb and found that the great stone guarding the entrance was rolled away. The tomb was empty.

To help us understand the scriptures, we want to teach you a song and show you some illustrations we have made of this story.

Child Reader: Luke 24:1-2.
(*pictures made by the children in section 1 of the mural*)
Sing: "The Stone Is Rolled Away"
Child Reader: Luke 24:3-6.
(*pictures made by the children in section 2 of the mural*)
Sing: "The Stone Is Rolled Away"
Child Reader: Luke 24:6b-9.
(*pictures made by the children in section 3 of the mural*)
Sing: "The Stone Is Rolled Away"
Child Reader: Luke 24:10.
(*pictures made by the children in section 4 of the mural*)
Sing: "The Stone Is Rolled Away"
Child Reader: Luke 24:11-12.
(*pictures made by the children in section 5 of the mural*)
Sing: "The Stone Is Rolled Away"

Leader tells cut-paper story.

Symbols are signs that remind us of something. We have many symbols that remind us of this wonderful Easter story.
(*cut out paper egg*)

What is this, boys and girls?
(*have children reply throughout; add egg*)

Eggs remind us of the Easter story because out of a dead thing, a shell, comes a living bird, the miracle of life. We all shall die, but out of our death shall come a new wonderful life.
(*cuts again, this time an Easter lily*)

What is this?
(*an Easter lily*)

Once this was a hard brown bulb with a papery shell that was buried in the earth. Now it is a beautiful lily. This too reminds us of the Easter story.
(*cut again, this time a butterfly*)

What is this?

(*a butterfly*)

You know the life cycle of a butterfly. First it is a cat-erpillar, then it wraps itself in a cocoon and emerges as a beautiful butterfly. This is like Jesus who lived, died, and rose again to life.

(*cuts again, this time the sun*)

Who can tell what this is?

(*the sun*)

Every evening the sun goes down and rises again at dawn. So Jesus died and rose again.

(*Have four pieces of paper folded and taped together so that they can be unfolded one at a time, accordion-like.*)

Here is God's message about death.

Sheet 1 — God is (*unfold next sheet*)

Sheet 2 — God loves us. (*unfold next sheet*)

Sheet 3 — God is greater than we are. (*unfold next sheet*)

Sheet 4 — We can trust God. (*spread out all four sheets and stand the picture up*)

Closing Hymn: "Christ The Lord Is Risen Today"

Children shake small bells on "Alleluia."

* *The Family Discovers the Meaning of Easter; Jesus Lives* pp. 38-40 by Charles Butts (Boston, MA: Pilgrim Press, 1960); edited by Hazel and Ted Schonmaker, Oliver Powell and Alice Goddard.

Tower of Pride

Preparation for the Service

Music is an important part of all liturgies. The opening hymn for this liturgy praises the God of all creation. The Shaker hymn "Simple Gifts" captures the theme and the other songs suggested are familiar to most children: "Lord I Want To Be A Christian" and "He's Got The Whole World In His Hands." Always feel free to substitute songs and hymns from your tradition.

Children have encountered pride. They have known people who are boastful and conceited. This service looks at what the Bible tells us about this trait, in the context of the Christian community.

To Prepare

1. Choose a child reader for Bible reading and prayer.
2. Choose six children for remembering people with special gifts.
3. Choose a soloist for Shaker hymn "Simple Gifts" available on the web and Youtube.
4. The sermon is a participation drama featuring a reader, costumed pantomime characters, and the participation of the entire congregation. The reader tells the story and directs the congregation in its participation. A child can play the part of King Nimrod, richly costumed as a mighty king. Another child, with musical experience, can be the drummer who accompanies King Nimrod, setting the pace of this story by the rhythm of his drumbeat (slow and steady when the king is in procession; fast and frantic when confusion hits Babel). Any number of children can act as captured soldiers. They process slowly and leave their swords at Nimrod's feet. It is most effective if they are all costumed

differently, suggesting different tribes and cities captured by Nimrod. Children taking part in the participation drama will need to rehearse. The part of the congregation will be spontaneous and unrehearsed. There should be a chair at the front of the church for Nimrod's throne and you may want to include a backdrop.

5. Cards and pencils should be available for every person attending the service.

Order of Service

Opening Hymn: "Let All The World In Every Corner Sing"

Responsive Sentences

Bible Reading

Prayer

Song: "Lord, I Want To Be A Christian In My Heart"

Meditation on Using Gifts

Solo: "Simple Gifts"

Participation Drama: Tower of Pride

Dedication Cards

Closing Hymn: "He's Got The Whole World In His Hands"

Leader: Welcome to our children's liturgy. Today we are going to experience a story based on one of the oldest stories in our Bible. This story was told many years before it was written down. It is a story about pride, and the message is just as true for us as for those ancient listeners. Let us worship together and learn from our scriptures.

Opening Hymn: "Let All The World In Every Corner Sing"

Responsive Sentences

Leader: Make a joyful noise unto the Lord, all ye lands.

Congregation: It is he that has made us and not we ourselves.

Leader: Serve the Lord with gladness; come before his presence with singing.

Congregation: It is he that has made us and not we ourselves.

Leader: Know ye that the Lord is God.

Congregation: We are his people and the sheep of his pasture.

Leader: Enter into his gates with thanksgiving and into his courts with praise; be thankful to him and bless his name.

Congregation: It is he that has made us and not we ourselves.

Leader: For the Lord is good, his mercy is everlasting, and his truth endureth to all generations.

Congregation: It is he that has made us and not we ourselves.

Leader: "It is he that has made us and not we ourselves." Today we come together to think about pride. The dictionary says that pride is "too high an opinion of one's self or too high an opinion of one's worth or possessions." God wants us to be proud of ourselves and the talents and gifts God has given us, but God doesn't want us to be scornful of others or vain or arrogant.

Child Reader: Listen to what the Bible says, Romans 12:3: "For by the grace given to me I say to everyone among you not to think of yourself more highly than you ought to think, but to think with sober judgment, each according to the measure of faith that God has assigned."

Prayer (*led by child*)
For the times we have been proud, Father, forgive us. For the times we have been conceited, Father, forgive us. For the times we have made fun of others, Father, forgive us. For the times we have hurt others, Father, forgive us. Amen.

Leader: Jesus Christ has come to forgive our pride and to make us his servants who live and build for the Lord.

Song: "Lord, I Want To Be A Christian In My Heart"

Leader: All things come from the creative and loving power of God. God has given to all of us special gifts and talents. But sometimes we don't use God's gifts in the right way, or we don't use them at all. Let's think now about people with special gifts from God and how they can use their gifts to God's glory.

Child 1: I'm thinking about the leaders of our country. May they use their talents for world peace.
Child 2: I'm thinking about doctors and nurses. May they use their talents to heal people.
Child 3: I'm thinking about ministers and church school teachers. May they use their talents to teach and show us God's way.

Child 4: I'm thinking about artists and musicians. May they use their talents to bring beauty into our lives.

Child 5: I'm thinking about scientists and researchers. May they help us understand our world.

Child 6: I'm thinking about firemen and policemen. May they help us have a safe community.

Leader: Can you think of others — people with special gifts that can be used to help others?

I'm thinking about children who use their eyes to see when they can help and their ears to hear when mother or father calls and makes everyone in the family glad. Others? (*accept suggestions from congregation*)

Solo: "Simple Gifts"

Leader: Our sermon today is based on Genesis 11:1-9, a story from the Old Testament. To make the story more meaningful, I am going to ask you to help me tell it. It is the story of the tower of pride.

Many years had passed after the great flood when Noah had saved all of his family and all of the animals from destruction. The sons of Noah had sons of their own and these married and had children. Soon there were a large number of people on earth and they all spoke the same language.

They chose a king from among themselves. His name was King Nimrod.

(*king enters down aisle in costume; he is accompanied by drummer beating slow march to which they walk; when king reaches front, leader speaks*)

Leader: (*to congregation*) This is your King Nimrod and all of you are the people of Babel. Rise and bow to your king.

(*congregation bows and then sits*)

Leader: In many ways King Nimrod was a good king, but he had one fault. He was too proud. He looked around to all the people whom he ruled and decided that they were a very great people and needed a fine city in which to live. And so they built a city. King Nimrod looked at the city. "Surely this is the best city anywhere around," he said. "It is big and it is strong and it has high walls and great towers and strong gates. We will call it Babel." And his pride grew a little more. "We are surely the best," he said, and all the people agreed. Will you all nod your heads in agreement?

(*congregation nods*)

King Nimrod became a king mighty in battle and he conquered other cities and lands far and wide.

(*soldiers in differing costumes enter from rear and place their swords at King Nimrod's feet and exit*)

But of all the cities he ruled, Babel was the largest and richest, and the people of Babel knew it.

The king's confidence in his own wisdom increased. He became cruel and domineering. He forgot that all gifts come from God.

"I need a mighty palace," he said, and they built a palace for the king that was greater and richer and mightier than any other palace. "It is surely the best," the king said, and all the people agreed.

For a while the king and the people were content with the greatest city and the greatest army and the greatest palace.

But a desire entered the king's soul to make himself greater even than God. "I will build a great tower," he said, "that will reach all the way to heaven. And I shall climb to the top of that tower and be mightier than God."

So the king went out among his people.

(*king walks down aisle accompanied by drummer*)

He selected some people from Babel to choose the site of his great tower.

(*king motions for them to stand up; the group he indicates should be about one half of the right side of the congregation*)

He chose more people to draw the plans.

(king motions the second half of the right side to stand)

These people were proud of their superior ability and dazzling brilliance. Will the rest of you (congregation on left) stand and bow to these people?

(king motions them all to be seated)

They chose a site and planned a tower whose base was larger than the city itself.

The king was very pleased and he went out among the people again.

(king walks into congregation accompanied by drummer)

He chose from among his people those who would chop straw and mix it with clay and mold and fire the bricks.

(king motions for half of the left side of the congregation to stand)

He chose others to put the plan together, and these people were extremely proud of their excellent bricks and were sure they were the best craftsmen ever known. (last half of the left section stands) Will the rest of you (congregation on right) please stand and bow to these excellent craftsmen?

And each group was sure that they were more important than all the rest. The tower began to grow, and grow, and grow. But the king wasn't satisfied. "Higher! Higher!" he shouted. "Work faster! Work harder! We'll be greater than God. We must reach the heavens before we stop."

(drum beats faster and harder)

The tower grew higher and higher until its top disappeared in the clouds.

God watched the mad ambition of King Nimrod and his people and decided to teach them a lesson. This is what God did: He started them all speaking different languages. Suddenly each man found that he could not understand what anyone else was saying. Will the Group 1 people please stand up? (first half of right side of congregation) All they could say was, "Chatter! Chatter!" The king ran among them, and

this is what happened when they tried to speak to him.
(*people say, "Chatter! Chatter!"*)

Will the people in Group 2 please stand up? (second half of right side of congregation) All you can say is, "Twaddle! Twaddle!" The king ran to them, but this is what happened when they tried to speak to him.
(*people say, "Twaddle! Twaddle!"*)

Will the people in Group 3 speak stand up? (first half of left side of congregation) All you can say is "Gibber! Gibber!" The king ran to them, but this is what happened when they tried to speak to him.
(*people say, "Gibber! Gibber!"*)

Will the people in Group 4 please stand up? (second half of left side of congregation) All you can say is, "Quibble! Quibble!" The king ran to them, and this is what happened when they tried to speak to him.
(*people say, "Quibble! Quibble!"*)

And suddenly everyone was talking at once, and it sounded like this: (*Chatter — Twaddle — Gibber — Quibble; all groups talk at the same time*)

Now we know why today the word "babel" means confusion.

Well, the tower was never finished. People who spoke the same language grouped together and moved away. They tilled new land, founded new cities. The population was dispersed over the face of the whole earth. They scattered everywhere.

King Nimrod had no people to rule. He was no longer proud. Too late he realized that all things come from the creative and loving power of God.
(*king and drummer leave*)

And the tower crumbled and fell to pieces. Some people say that even today on the banks of the Euphrates River you can still see a pile of stone and rubble as high as a mountain that once was the great tower of Babel that reached to the clouds.

Leader: It seems silly that someone would try to build a tower all the way to God. But every time we do something out of pride instead of love of God, we are doing the same thing. Let's think about some of these things now.

(*accept answers from congregation*)

Now let's think of something we can do to show the love of God. In your seats is a card. Will you write a word or draw a picture that shows something you can do to show your love of God? When you have finished, bring these cards and leave them at the altar.

Father, accept these offerings, accept us, and use us for your purpose.

Closing Hymn: "He's Got The Whole World In His Hands"

What Does God Expect of Me?

Preparation for the Service

This children's liturgy seeks to help children understand that even they, at their early stage of life, can make a commitment and dedicate themselves to God.

To Prepare

This service will need children with some acting ability. The sermon/monologue should be given by a young boy with a good speaking voice and the ability to convince the audience that he is, indeed, the "boy with the loaves and fishes."

In addition, the skit "The Stone in the Road" uses eight child actors who all have speaking parts. These are:

• the king
• two servants of the king
• two men of the village
• two women of the village
• boy (or girl) of the village

There are two important props in the skit: a large stone made of papier-mache or something similar and a bag of gold. The characters may wear costumes. This skit will need to be rehearsed a number of times.

The ropes used in the dedication chain may either be plain rope or a more formal, fancy type of rope found at a fabric shop.

Order of Service

Unison Call to Worship

Opening Hymn: "For The Beauty Of The Earth"

Scripture

Skit: "The Stone in the Road"

Unison Prayer

Hymn: "This Little Light Of Mine"

Sermon/Monologue

Make Dedication Chain

Leader: Welcome to our children's liturgy. We have come together this morning to worship God. We have a theme. We have a printed service. But remember, worship is not a theme or a place or an order. Worship is what happens between God and us. Let us prepare now to worship God. First let us praise him.

Unison Call to Worship
Let us worship and bow down.
Let us kneel before the Lord our maker.
For he is our God and we are his children.
Today, let us hear his voice and turn our hearts toward him.
(adapted from Psalm 95:6-8)

Opening Hymn: "For The Beauty Of The Earth"

Leader: Today I want you to think about a question: What does God expect of me? We usually know what our parents expect or what our teachers expect, but what does God expect of us? What can we give? We are just children, what have we to offer?

Jesus told us a story that answers that question:

Luke 21:1-4 (read by child or told as a story)

Leader: Later, after the time of Jesus when the apostles were carrying on his work, we find another story that helps us answer the question: What does God expect of us?

Acts 3:1-10 (read by child or told as a story)

Leader: "Gold and silver have I none, but what I have I give."

Now we are going to see a skit that answers the same question.

Skit: "The Stone in the Road"

(*king walks down aisle in crown and robe, he is accompanied by two friends and as he enters he speaks*)

King: I am very worried about the people of my kingdom.

Friend 1: Yes, O king.

King: They leave everything to me.

Friend 2: Yes, O king.

King: No one in this whole kingdom seems to try to do anything for themselves. Am I right?

Friends: (*together*) Yes, O king.

King: (*has reached front of church, faces audience*) I think it is time to teach them a lesson. You (*points to Friend 1*) go and find me the biggest rock you can find.

(*Friend 1 exits to left*)

You (*points to Friend 2*) dig me a hole, here in the middle of the road. (*Friend 2 pantomimes digging, Friend 1 returns with huge rock*)

King: Now here is my plan. (*takes bag of gold from his pocket*) I will place this gold in this hole and cover it with this large rock. As my people pass, I will watch and see if any will move the rock and find the gold. Come on, let's hide.

(*King and Friend 1 and Friend 2 hide behind the pulpit and peek out*)

(*two men enter*)

Man 1: What's this? A big rock in the middle of the road!

Man 2: How will we get our carts around it when we take our vegetables to market?

Man 1: The king should know about this!

Man 2: I certainly hope someone tells him.

(*men exit*)

King: Ah ha! Just as I expected!

(*two women enter*)

Woman 1: Will you look at this? A rock in the middle of the road!

Woman 2: This is an outrage! Our community is going to pieces.

Woman 1: Something must be done about this.

Woman 2: The authorities should be notified.

(*two women exit*)

King: Do you see what I mean? Do you see?

Friend 1 and Friend 2: Yes, O king.

(*boy enters*)

Boy: What's this? It is a big rock in the middle of the road. This is dangerous. Someone might get hurt. I'll see if I can move it. (*Boy strains against rock*) There, I did it. Now no one will get hurt. But what's this? A bag of gold? (*picks up bag*) I must return this to the king.

(*King steps out from behind pulpit*)

King: At last I've found someone who can do something for himself.

Boy: Sir, anyone could have moved that rock.

King: Anyone could do it, but only you did it. The gold is yours.

(*King, Friend 1, Friend 2, Boy, and rock exit*)

Leader: Let us pray:

For the times I have run away from the things I should have done, Father, forgive me. For choosing the easy way out instead of the helpful way, Father, forgive me. For leaving stones in the road that I could have moved, Father, forgive me. Open my eyes to the needs around me that I can meet. Amen.

Hymn: "This Little Light Of Mine"

Leader: Have you been thinking about our question: What does God expect of me? Are you beginning to get some ideas for an answer? A poet once said, "Our grand business is not

to see what lies dimly at a distance, but to do what lies clearly at hand." Are we ready to answer the question now?
(*boy from audience*)
Before we do, can I say something?
Leader: Well, I suppose so. Who are you?
(*boy comes into pulpit*)

Sermon/Monologue

I am just a boy, a boy who lived in Jesus' day; but I had an experience that told me what God expected of me.

It all began like any other day. My mother rose very early that morning as she always does. At about four in the morning, your time, all the women of the village gather at the community oven to bake the family's bread for the day. I went with her that day to watch. I love to watch them baking bread. It starts as a small ball of dough which is patted into a horizontal cake. Then the cake is picked up and swirled, growing steadily larger and thinner, until it is just right. My mother is very good at this, but when I asked her to let me try, my bread fell in a lump. Mother just laughed and picked it up again. When she had it just the right size she plopped it into the oven and made some more loaves. It cooked for just a few minutes, and then it was baked and oh, did it smell good. Try to imagine what it looked like. It wasn't shaped like your bread, but was a flat sheet about a quarter of an inch thick. It was dark brown in color. Mother made lots of loaves. Then we stacked them up and brought them home, hot and steaming and crusty. Mother put aside five of the loaves for my lunch.

Our house would seem funny to you. We just had one room, so our kitchen where mother put the bread was also our living room.

We ate mostly bread for all our meals, but we had a few other things too. That day we had some fish in the house. This fish came from the Sea of Galilee and it had been dried in the hot sun several days before. Mother packed two of the small, dried fish in my lunch. I like to eat and I thought this was a great lunch for my day.

Where was I going that day? Out on the hillside to hear Jesus. My whole family was going and so were all of our neighbors. Mother had fixed me a lunch of my own in case we became separated. And it was a good thing she did, because so many people came to hear Jesus that I soon wandered away from my family to be with my friends, and I kept edging closer to the front. You know, like you do at parades.

It was a marvelous day. Jesus is so kind and wise and all his disciples were there around him. Sometimes we sat on a hillside and listened to Jesus and sometimes we followed Jesus as he walked. The sky was blue and the wild flowers were blowing in a gentle breeze and scented the air. We stayed on and on and forgot the time and forgot to eat. Before we realized it, it was getting late. I was near Jesus and heard his disciples talking. Peter said, "Master, we are five miles from the nearest village and the people are getting restless and hungry." Philip said, "It wouldn't matter if we were near a market. It would take hundreds of dollars to feed this many people. There must be 5,000 people here." Jesus smiled, "Ask them all to sit down," he said. "There's plenty of grass. They need to rest." Some of the people began to mutter as the disciples seated them, "I'm hungry, I want to go home."

I don't know why I did it. The disciples seemed so anxious. I heard a baby cry out in hunger. Anyway, I took my lunch to Jesus — the five fresh barley loaves and the two dried fish. Jesus smiled at me. I think I stuttered, "Master, if this is any use to you — I thought — I mean —." I handed him my lunch. I thought at first I had done a dumb thing.

But then the miracle happened. I still don't know why or how, but Jesus took my lunch and blessed it and passed it out to the people and it was enough. All those who were hungry that day were fed and Jesus said to his disciples, "It isn't the rich who give us of their riches, but the simple-hearted who give all that they have."

I had such a small thing to give, but I gave it anyway, and it was just what Jesus wanted. If God could do that with my lunch, what can he do with your gifts — with your brains maybe or your talents. Who knows? Are you willing to try?

Leader: What does God expect of you? At our altar we have a piece of rope. In my hand I have many small pieces of rope. If you are willing, like the boy with the loaves and fishes, to offer whatever you have to God, will you come forward? I will give you a small piece of rope and you may tie your piece to the rope on the altar. We will form a chain of dedication.
(*after all have done this*)
Leader: Go in peace and may you always live as God expects you to live. Amen.

About the Author

Judy Gattis Smith is a teacher, author, and workshop leader. She has written eighteen books in the field of Christian education and has worked professionally as a local church Christian educator. Judy has traveled extensively leading over 200 workshops and classes for churches of various denominations.

Among her honors are "Mother of the Year for Religious Activities," Roanoke, Virginia; and "Outstanding Christian Educator Award" from the Christian Educators Fellowship of the United Methodist Church of the Virginia Conference. Upon her retirement, she was awarded a "Lifetime Achievement Award" for distinguished leadership in the ministry of Christian education.

Judy and her husband, a retired Methodist minister, live in Midlothian, Virginia. They have two adult children and four granddaughters.